C000145369

# Otherwise Engaged

A Literature and Arts Journal
Volume 6. Winter 2020.
Quarantine Edition II

Edited and Compiled

by Marzia Dessi

# ARTISTS AND WRITERS

A Whittenberg
AE Reiff
Anagha Joy
Anannya Dasgupta
Ann Privateer
B.A. Brittingham
Beatrice Georgalidis
Bill Cushing
Bransha Gautier
Bruce McRae
C. Rose Widmann
Carl "Papa" Palmer
Carmen Caro
Catherine Alexander
Chahat Soneja
CJP Lee
Dave Medd
David Subacchi
Dee Allen
Derek Roper
Douglas K Currier
Dr. Emily Bilman
Dr. Shubha Dwivedi
Elena Brooke
Eva Eliav
F. Berna Uysal,
Faruk Buzhala
Guilherme Bortoluzzi
Helga Grundler-Schierloh
Jaina Cipriano
Jan Ball
JBMulligan
Jeanette Willert
Jeffrey G. Delfin
Jenn Powers
John Tavares

Jude Brigley
K. P. Heyming
K.A. Johnson
Karol Nielsen
Kelli J Gavin
Lee Ellis
Linda Imbler
Linda M. Crate
Lorraine Caputo
M. A. Blickley
Madeleine McDonald
Mae Tanes Espada
Mark A. Fisher
Mark Andrew Heathcote
Martin Eastland
Matthew Kerr
Mike L. Nichols
Neal Amandus Gellaco
Ololade Akinlabi Ige
Peniel Gifted
Perla Kantarjian
Rachel Makinson
RAMEEZ AHMAD BHAT
Rob Mimpriss
Robert Cooperman
Rp Verlaine
Ruchira Mandal
Shaista Fazal
Shannon Frost Greenstein
Sohini Shabnam
Stephen Craig Finlay
Steven Rossi
Sumati Muniandy
Swarnav Misra
Tal Garmiza
Tali Cohen Shabtai
Thomas Zampino
William Barker
Yeshi Choden

# Between us Exists Universes

By K.P. Heyming

Between us exists universes
only ever joined by the stardust
of our fingertips. This chaotic chasm
of space lingers,
waiting for a cataclysm
to bring us together
or to tear us apart
so that we may be reborn
into a galaxy we knew would survive us.
Let our atoms return to each other
having once delighted in comfortable company
before the big bang threw us into lives
that were not made to be separate.
Let this space between us
disappear like the one we've forgotten
we're made of, and let these stardust fingertips
intertwine with yours
so that they may remember
what being whole feels like again.

# Sophmores

By Jenn Powers

# Arica Morn

By Lorraine Caputo

To the morning twilight I
awaken, Mars a
crimson speck on the not-yet
clouded sky

& the briny aroma
of the sea drifts through
the still city streets to this
balcony

# Family Silver

by Jan Ball

She's glad she got the silver
not the house, Thanksgiving,
and Christmases embedded
in the luster of the spoons.
As children, they pierced
shrimp with the little shellfish
forks then poked through
the cream on top of slices
of pumpkin pie with salad
forks washed after the waldorf
salad, reappearing magically
for dessert.

She's glad she got the silver
not the house, so she can
show it off tonight at the dinner
party for her Boston friends,
first figs stuffed with prosciutto,
bleu cheese and basil, then Bob's
asparagus soup and wagyu beef
roast with a montage of veges.

She has taken out the silver knives
from the set Aunt Kate gave Dad
for his first marriage, took them
back when he divorced, then
gave them to Mom when Dad
married her. In the family for fifty
years, her guests now spread soft
brie on their French bread then
later use the silver forks to eat
the apple crumble she's prepared.

She's glad she got the silver not
the house. "You already have a house,"
her mother told her as she handed her
the silver. Her sister had to sell
the house, but she still has the silver.

# Learning is not that easy

By Jeanette Willert

The cast iron skillet looks benign
 lying bottom up on the kitchen floor.  Nor,
does the greenish olive oil pooled around its rim
sound any alarm. My right foot,
at this moment, would disagree.

A minute ago (though pain registers time
differently than a watch) the frying pan
slipped from my grip.  Gravity,
having its way, aimed at and hit my big toe.
A thankful note is due…the pan
had not yet touched the waiting burner
nor been filled with seasoned trout.

Without a doubt, my brain
registers what my body knows: bones
are broken.  How many in a toe?
Then, when the curses stop streaming,
a pause, a breath, to acknowledge pain.

Life happens that way, doesn't it?
an action that cannot be recalled,
a recognition flickers,
 a consequence commences:
                        sometimes a joy,
                        sometimes a debt,
                        but, often, a hurt.
From these, legend claims we learn.

Yet, legends and fables, like fairy tales,
flirt with truth, sound convincing.
Odds are, Hansel and Gretel were
as cooked as last Sunday's roast.

# Amanda on Teaching

By John Grey

Teaching takes four eyes, six hands.
So says Amanda.
The loudly spoken equivalent
of a ruler on the knuckles
is not part of her method.
Rote is not to her liking.
And mentally dismembering children
is unacceptable in any profession,
which is why she is a teacher.

The curriculum is bunk
with its dumb and hidebound posturing.
So she is somewhat of a Zen master.
Her point is that
what is unknowable
is inexhaustible in the approaches
of not knowing it.
She has a knack of answering a question
with a prayer.

As for her pupils, all are wanting.
And she leaves for home some nights
to the sound of her heels on cold cement
like one hand clapping.
She wishes she had
that second set of eyes
to offset the ones that tear up at night.

She tries to teach poetry.
A boy asks if there is any money in it.
Then there is a tantrum from one kid
as if the classroom is a supermarket aisle,
and Amanda his bedraggled mother.

Some haven't had their breakfasts.
One likes to use the word 'fag'
in describing those he doesn't get along with.
None look as if they want to be here.
She is like a runner
in the lane with impossible wind resistance.

She begins to thank God for recess.
For there's no place in these hearts and heads for
Blake's fiery visions,
Dickinson's modest wisdom,
Whitman's humanism,
Wordsworth's wellspring of imagination,
John Keats' empirical romance.
Poets lack for air in classrooms.
They suffocate on the page.

Miracles take more than patience.
A superior being is required.
Amanda can't walk on water.
Nor give sight to the blind.
She considers herself devoted and good.
Never charming and intelligent.
Her pride wouldn't stand for it.

Nothing helps.
So many in her care remained totally ignorant
of just about everything
and determined to stay that way.

Amanda scours the want-ads.
Maybe there is something else for her out there.
To her dismay, she finds nothing.
Then she watches TV and nibbles on a frozen dinner.
There has been a terrible earthquake in South America.
Many died.
And then there is a show about a rich woman

who fired her cook in a pique
and has to prepare a meal for fifteen herself.
The dying, the prideful – these are different lives.
Not hers.

Tomorrow, it's back to the blackboard.
She still has only two hands, two eyes.
She remembers the proverb,
"In teaching others, we teach ourselves."
So the kids would be getting a dumb instructor.
They'd just have to do a better job of teaching her.

# Winter's Bones

By C. Rose Widmann

My footsteps crunch in the old snow,
And breath mists out like billowing smoke.
My usual haunt is shrouded in ice,
Barely recognizable even to this regular spectre.

The trees are like skeletal fingers,
Reaching up from the cold Earth.
Clawing, beckoning, screaming,
To the crescent moon.

My shrouded form parts the mist,
Slithering material joining whispers from the trees.
The longing for summer's comfort,
Is long since resting in peace.

Should my soul cut its earthly ties,
And be with winter's bones once more?

# Winter's Bones

By C. Rose Widmann

# The Room
By Emily Bilman

The brown leather gloves on the desk
hard-swollen in their knuckles shone
with the sun's half-light as if they could not
contain the guilty pleasures of the criminals.
The room looked cozy yet felt quite cold
as if the darkness of the human soul
had hallowed the author's soul. Harrowed
was his heart with his characters' remorse

in his writing room that became a museum.
The atmosphere fomented with anxiety
inside the room as into my troubled
consciousness waiting for redemption
his leather gloves filled with grief burst
their hard seams of delinquent guilt.

# Rescue

By Robert Cooperman

In the Safeway parking lot, he was hulking
over your car; he wore a cutaway tank top
that boasted his biceps and ripped abs; he sported
a thug-Mullet; a cigarette scowled his mouth.

"Look what you did to my car, old man!"
he towered over you like a threatening
border guard and pointed to a scratch.

"Get lost," you hissed. "This piece-a crap
wasn't parked here when I pulled in."

"You did this, you pay," he poked
a silencer-thick forefinger at your chest.

"Back off," you rasped and aimed
your cane under his nose, Louise exiting
the store with some forgotten items.

"Ralph!" she shrieked, "stop
bothering that nice young man!
Please excuse my husband," she patted
the kid's arm, "he's not himself."
Once inside the car, Louise spat,

"You dope!  If the cops'd shown up
and nosed around the trunk
we'd have been in cuffs.
Now drive!"

# Lucifers
## by K.A. Johnson

John was outside the meeting lodge that abutted the lake.
Almost everyone else was inside conversing and having a
good time. John had never fit in at White Pine Lodge. It was
an academic summer camp for rich kids. John was not rich,
and the other kids knew that. His aunt had paid for him
feeling it would help John in his studies and as she put it
"growth into being a young gentleman." John was playing
with his lucifers. He liked the garlic smell that came when the
white phosphorus ignited. He loved how the flame danced in
the dwindling light. William, his only friend at White Pine
Lodge, came over to him, startling him. John thought
William had been inside with everyone else at the end of the
summer get together. William was the only one who didn't
seem to care that John wasn't rich and treated him like he did
everyone else at the camp.

"You shouldn't play with those," William said.
"Matches are dangerous."

"Why aren't you inside with everyone else, all your
other friends?" John responded.

"I was looking for you, come in, have fun, it is the
end of the summer."

"I don't want to see them."

"Have it your way, but maybe if you tried, you would
fit in better," William said while turning to head to the door.
John struck another lucifer; the tip crumbled sending flaming
balls into the ground. One ignited some dried pine needles
by the lodge. John turned white, he tried to step on the
flame, but it kept growing; the dried pine needles made loud
popping noises as they quickly caught flame spreading the
fire. John turned, and he ran. His shoes were biting into the
packed dirt of the old raised bed where the abandoned
original railroad track had once run before it was changed to
the new narrow gauge tracks — his heart racing from fear.

Tears started to stream down his dirt-streaked face — a salty taste when they ran over his lips into his mouth.

John was sure that William would tell that he was the one who was playing with matches. John was panting; he knew he couldn't run much further. He could hear screams in the distance. He knew they were looking for him and that William had already told on him. John veered off the railroad bed almost tripping on a fallen tree limb. Up a slight incline was a large rock. John scurried up to it. The rock rose high enough that John knew he could hide behind it and not be seen from the old railroad bed. Panting, he fell behind the sizeable jutting rock. Tears still rolled down his face. His skin hurt where branches had ripped into them. Sobbing uncontrollably he hid behind the rock. In the distance, John heard faint screams. As the last of the sun went down, John saw a soft glow in the sky from the direction of White Pine Lodge. John fell asleep to the sounds of loons yodeling to each other on the lake.

*The Bangor Daily Whig & Courier*
August 25, 1899
Twenty-six die in youth camp fire
by Samuel Henderson
Twenty four youths and two adults are assumed to have died yesterday in a fire at White Pine Lodge. The fire had been spotted by a conductor for the Bucksport and Bangor Railroad Company. The fire started in the early evening and quickly engulfed the meeting lodge by Tern Lake. The building burned to the ground. The fire was fast burning and hot cremating the bodies. The

cause of the fire is still under
investigation.

John woke up cold and shivering the next morning. His
body was stiff from sleeping on the ground. He went down
to the lake for a drink of water. He foraged in the woods for
food. He spent the night behind the rock again. A few days
later, tired of sleeping outside and hungry John decided to
return to White Pine Lodge. He made his way back down the
old railroad bed. He figured after being missing for several
days that the director would no longer be mad that he had
been playing with matches and would just be relieved that he
had been found safe. John ran to White Pine Lodge and
stopped abruptly. The meeting lodge where they had
gathered by the lake was gone. The stone chimney, covered
in black soot, and the concrete pad on which it stood
remained along with some unrecognizable rubble. The trees
around where the lodge had been were blackened. Then John
noticed that White Pine Lodge was utterly silent. He looked
around, not only was the meeting lodge gone but so was
everyone at the camp. John screamed out, "Hello." No
response came. He screamed out " Hello" again, his voice
quivering — still nothing. John's heart sank. They had left
him alone.
John spent the night in his old cabin. His stuff still there.
The next day he foraged through the camp for supplies.
Nothing had been taken. Food was plentiful. John didn't
know exactly where the camp was, nor how to find
civilization from it. When the summer began, he had arrived
by train on the new track at a stop just for the camp. It
wasn't a routine stop; the train only stopped there to drop off
the campers and staff then pick them up at the end of the
season. During the rest of the year, the train just flew
through without even slowing down.
John survived the cold New England winter, alone,
living off of the supplies in the camp. There was enough
food to last for ages, enough blankets, sleeping bags, and

pillows to stay warm. The cabin walls protected him from the harshest of the winter weather. In the Spring, as the snow began to melt, John got excited expecting the return of the staff, of new students. Spring came and went; no one showed up at the camp. John, not knowing what else to do, stayed. Another season came and went. No one arrived again.

Cabins started being built along the lake, scattered from each other. John would watch in hiding as they were built. Men ripped through logs with large saws. They would pull up a skeleton of the building, and throughout the summer, it would transform into a cabin. John didn't approach anyone; he was scared. But John learned how to sneak in and out of the newly built cottages, to steal food, so as to continue to survive in his little cabin at the abandoned summer camp. No one who was moving in along the lake ever ventured down that far and found his home.

Soon rumors started along the lake of a ghost that inhabited the lake. People would return to their cabin and find stuff had been moved and some food was missing. But no trace of a person was ever seen. Word started to spread that it was the ghost of a camper that had died in a fire that had occurred years before. The story grew and became lake legend.

The boat sat motionless on the glassy lake, the tracks where her paddles had struck the lake along with the wake where the canoe had split the water were gone. The lake was still and quiet. An occasional water strider, a bug from the Gerridae family, walked by on the water, striding, important, showing off that it was above falling through the water into the lake. Margaret looked toward shore. The cabin, owned by her parents, was barely visible through the thick trees. Several others were visible from where she sat. Several years ago, she thought, this lake had been almost uninhabited. Now, cabins were starting to pop-up all over. The vast land had been owned by an educational summer camp for overly rich and overly smart kids she had heard. Then something had happened, and the camp had closed. Her parents had mentioned that down the lake, the remnants still stood, but she had been told not to venture there. The remnants were of unknown condition, and it wouldn't be proper for her, a young woman, to be messing around there. She saw a flash of an object on the porch of their cabin. A glimpse that reminded her of a bear, that she had seen in pictures, but upright. Then it was gone.

Margaret paddled into shore, tied up the canoe and went up to the cabin. Her parents were coming down the dirt drive in their 1914 Chevrolet Baby Grand. She met them by the porch, and they went in together. The kitchen was in disarray, food spread around. Margaret looked at her dad and told him about the bear. He shook his head. It is the ghost he said, the spirit of a boy who died at the summer camp when a fire had burned most of the campers alive.

Margaret sat in an aging lawn chair by the campfire outside her cabin, which she had inherited from her parents. Her daughter, Eileen, and grandchildren, Annie and Billy, were also seated around the fire. The faint tinny sound of "You're the One That I Want" by John Travolta, and Olivia Newton-John lightly floated through the air from a Sony CF-580 portable radio at a neighboring cabin. Eileen was engrossed in telling the story of the ghost of Tern Lake to Annie and Billy. They looked spooked as Eileen animatedly told the story.

"As they got closer, they saw a ghostly apparition slip shimmering through the woods away from the cabin disappearing among the trees. Rushing inside, they saw furniture was in disarray, and the fridge door was open," Eileen said.

A burst of arthritic pain jolted through Margaret pulling her from the story. There hadn't been any incidents of missing food for many years. Margaret thought back to the day she had seen the bear when she was younger. Ghost, her dad, had said but Margaret knew better. Most of the people along the lake that told the ghost story over the flickering light of a campfire didn't even date back to when the incidents had happened. White Pine Lodge had long since been demolished and turned into lakefront mini-mansions for the nouveau riche.

"What is that, shimmering in the woods behind you!" Eileen shouted pointing behind Annie and Billy.

Annie screamed, and Billy quickly turned peering off into the inky blackness of the woods around them. Margaret chuckled, one day Annie and Billy would be telling this same story to their children.

From the direction of the lake, Margaret heard a loon yodel.

## Ember Eyes
By K.P. Heyming

He saw embers where her eyes
should have been and a smile
where none should have been.
She came back darker
than her shadow, yet he could not see
where the light was coming from.
He thought perhaps from above,
had he not chanced a glance
behind and seen the carnage created
by this creature left unloved
for too long. He saw embers
where her eyes should have been
and an emptiness where none
should have been.

# Coal Chute

By B.A. Brittingham

# "Hunger"

By Mae Tanes Espada

*"Go on, do not stop touching yourself. Because in this world, no one is going to love you other than you and your dirty fingers."*

-

In a small, dim and dingy room, there is a girl touching herself with such fervor it is almost a case of molestation. She has small hands. She curls her hips in and out. This is her secret dance, the one she does not tell anyone about. The one she indulges in nightly and then shoves into the recesses of her mind until the next sundown. She does not tell her lovers about these rendezvous she has with her own body, her own acute awareness of what feels right. She does not tell them. They are scarecrows to her. They are sacks stuffed with cotton, stuffed with seed, which are meant to scare away her lust, but fail. She can kiss their mouths, oh yes. She can kiss their mouths and believe in it, but when she gets home and peels her clothes so lovingly away from her skin, she cannot help but realize the attraction she has for her own body, her body built like a mausoleum of bones.

-

*I remember the perennial and unforgiving silence.*

-

The girl is young. She does not want to be named. She has dark shoulder-length hair, a long bob. She is petite. She has pale skin. You can see her veins. She looks so delicate. She has small lips that rarely curves into a smile. At first glance she looks ordinary. Nothing very special about her. She looks like a kid. Looks too young for her age. Seems like someone who is forced to grow up too early. But when you look at her closely, that is when you will realize that there is something different about her: there is something about her eyes and the way she looks. Or stares. It is unsettling. Disturbing. One look from her and it feels like you are being stripped raw. No wonder she can drive people away or draw people in just by staring into her eyes.

-

*I remember my father's fingers, cold and trembling, tracing the outlines of my knuckles. I remember the eyes that dare not meet, nor chance a glimpse at the world that lived barred behind a pane of frosted glass. I remember the harsh cadence of rain that battered that glass, frantic like fists, demanding entry.*

-

She grew up in a family where people are always threatening to leave. A father who is more fingers and fists than man, a mother who is more eyes and hands than woman. Brother and sister who are more shadows than people. A father holding his wife's hands, with his eyes clinging to his daughter's nape, if she is as sweet as her mother, he wonders. A house, not a home. Walls that knew everything. A ceiling that saw everything. Pillows that knew the teeth, tears, blood, and nightmares. In this house, messages are not always read. And if they are, responses are not always found. In this house, you do not cry or else they will give you something to cry about. In this house, you bite down hard until you taste your own blood.

-

*I remember the taste of my own apprehension: bitter and pungent, a tang that lingered on my tongue despite my attempts to dilute it with the coffee I nursed.*

-

She imagines in the corner a dark thing with hunched shoulders and a wicked grin that urges her on. It is excitable. "Go on," it caws sweetly through the smell of smoke and damp, "touch your skin. See how it warms faster to your own hands than anyone else's. See how it yields!" And it is true. Deep down in the middle, she gives way to her own advances. Her fingers plunge easily into a world of velvet. And she is alive and she is ashamed all at once. She cannot believe the animation of her body, how it responds so quickly when the right parts are provoked. But she is guilty, too. She is horrified at her greed, at the way she prods and presses and fucks and breaks. How she then does it all over again. How the time she spends molding herself like clay drips by and by until she is drowning in a sea of wasted hours. Until her breath has been lost so many times she doubts its return is necessary.

-

*I remember the idle way my mother hand's worked cleaning the dishes. I remember how gingerly she stacked them, as if the subtle clamor of porcelain clattering together would break the solemnity of our vigil. I remember the slump of her shoulders; contemplating the futility of her actions. I remember wondering if we would need that china. I remember thinking it would not matter even if we did.*

-

For years she was lost between mistaking moths for pixies and the need to be an adult and carry on. She could not carry on so she whispered to the pixies instead. She quietly tried to untangle herself from ghosts, tried to tiptoe her way out but did not succeed for very long. She was followed by a storm of wasps having picked up the sweet scent of guilt and remorse, mistook her north for her west and ended up somewhere in the dark with her heart pretending to be a compass. She found it silly the way people still calculate things so wrongly in spite the lessons they have learned. She thought she could hide if she were smaller but some things are so big they always come find her even in the cracks.

-

*I remember my mother's suitcases packed by the door, her anger leaving her crumpled rather than mighty. I remember my father's mouth spraying spit across the living room, across all the living rooms in all the houses we ever lived. I remember my father - a giant gargoyle in front of the television, banishing everyone from the room with a turn of his head alone. My mother beating her head against the wall, the blood coming slowly. I remember the threats to leave. By him or her and then my siblings eventually, except they made good on their word.*

-

Still the thing in the corner, which breathes heavy as she breathes, which groans and moans as it watches her, it calls out more. It squawks loudly while she throws herself off the edge of sweet sin.

-

*I remember my brother's face, etched in stone. I remember my sister's incessant fidgeting.*

-

"Again!" it demands. "Do not stop. What else is there? What else is there besides this power at your own fingertips? You are a master in this world, in this world of sweat and stifled breaths and your breasts like peaches swollen with nectar. You own yourself. How you give and give yourself away. To bruised knuckles. To starved eyes. To mouths that try to suck you dry. Take yourself. Take, take," it presses. And she does. She does.

-

*I remember my brother abandoning one warzone for another, this time in uniform. This time with a squadron with whom he felt more at home. Even though they come after him during the night. This is better than nothing, is it not? My sister with a man whose wife was dying of leukemia. I was just trying to be of comfort, she would tell me. Then soon she would come with whoever who would take her, even with someone who gave her bruises on both the inside and out. And then there is me.*

-

Years later, they have asked the girl to forgive them for their silence, hold on to their hearts, like limp birds in her dried palms. Men have told her that she's beautiful because she can see their rocks as diamonds, and she listens to them in the dark. Yet rarely do these men imagine the weight of their brokenness, the fragility of the girl's body, her weariness from carrying their hearts and dragging her own. The girl has too many calluses on her hands from dragging oversized rib cages; and she's tired of carrying everything that is never her own. She wants to stop cradling their uncertainty as if there is not already too much of that in her. She wants to stop clinging on to men who are so silent and tough, whose voice she is so familiar with that she cannot block it even with her own screams.

-

*I remember the unvoiced questions that hung between us. I remember the foreboding uncertainty that loomed in the undisturbed quiet of our home. I remember the oppressive presence of dread that clung to the air, that served to calcify my lungs with every inhale. I remember the creeping atrophy in my muscles, the sharp pain that nestled itself in between the columns of my spine. I remember the electricity that thrummed through my veins. I remember my heart being driven by a weighted and erratic percussion, carried by a lamentation I dared not speak: I cannot.*

-

She is exhausted by the time she can take no more. She lies in sheets that swelter around her. She is throbbing at the center and may do so forevermore. She can hear nothing but the whirring of her own heart in the dark. All else is silence.

The girl looks back now. As a kid, the girl was never afraid of the dark. She slept under her sheets to avoid the whisper of the street lamps from the window. As a kid, she was never afraid of the dark. The most powerful gift she has been given are the words: "I see you," despite whatever name she chose to call herself. She has been afraid of the word "please" for so long that she forgot to notice that she still shakes. Her mother mistakes her pain for hatred. She begged mercy from her parents' embrace and spent years asking why.

-

*I remember the sound of rolling tires, the slap of boots, the thunderous bellow of voices.*

-

Even the demon is done for the night. He flashes a single satisfied smile and before fleeing the scene, he praises her: "You. Are. God."

-

*I remember the void that opened beneath us. I remember the tug. I remember the plummet.*

-

40

All the while the girl can hear the jangling of coins falling, falling, falling, as if it was the sound of eternal salvation. The girl can hear the crispness of fresh money, a sign of deliverance, of redemption.

-

*I remember being consumed.*

-

But tomorrow is another day and salvation is something that is far away, something that can be achieved – someday. But just not today. Because the show is not over until she has something to eat every supper.

-

*I remember that it hurts, but it hurts so good and besides, I have never known anything else. I take and eat everything with my own hands.*

-

The girl opens her eyes and stares into the screen. It is now her father she sees.

# Church-Mississippi

By B.A. Brittingham

# Smooth As Silk

By Martin Eastland

*New York City, 1926...*

HE FLOWED LIKE AIR, taking their wallets like a descending hawk snatches its prey. No one could touch him for his cunning and his light touch. Harley Leitman was the best pick-pocket in the city, and without peer. It was widely whispered he could walk three feet abreast and *still* take your wallet without your knowing it. The cops were useless, mostly due to the fact that the corruption rife in Tammany Hall was so pervading that they had become jaded, insisting they had bigger fish to fry than wasting time chasing some no-account street vagrant. The truth was that he was a non-entity, a small fish in a city full of *real* criminals, specifically those occupying Wall Street and the lower east side gangs who had organised themselves – including the indisputable fact that he remained faceless. No prints on file, no yellow sheet...no face, either. He was a ghost at best; an enigma in himself at worst.

The cobbled streets of the Lower East Side teemed with the lost and disenfranchised as they made their way through the grimy thoroughfare, their languorous pace and sullen faces betraying them as what they were. The lost and unwanted, citizens without a state, at least a state that gave a damn about them. Predominantly Jewish and Italian, they were immigrants from the first and second influx of European émigré. He watched them from a stoop as the rich ones made their way through the old neighborhood in their motorised carriages, their finery in full display despite grave warnings from the Police and friends in the same corrupt city government of which stock they were the same. But in the arrogance which their status afforded them, they didn't care, resolute in the misguided belief that they would be unmolested by the 'little people,' as long as they gave them a wide berth.

Leitman scoured the streets, taking in everything from the cut of their clothes, their facial hair, and their features, anything that would identify a viable target. "No point in risking capture for someone without a nickel to their name, is there?"

he would say to his friend and fellow pilferer, a young Sicilian boy called Enrico Villani. They had met in the school yard and became fast friends in those moments after. They would both soon be expelled from school and spent the days on the teeming streets, stealing wallets, purses and food from the stalls which lined the sidewalks. It was a good life – and a *lot* of fun. Until the day Rico – as he had become known – had been killed in a automobile accident escaping a more observant and relentless victim. He had run out of an alley into the throng and hadn't seen the dog catcher's van come out of nowhere. He had been pronounced dead at the scene. Harley could only watch in silenced horror as the cops surrounded his lifeless body, waiting for the meat-wagon to make its appearance. As they loaded his bagged corpse onto a gurney, and into the van, Harvey wept openly. His only friend gone forever. Harley knew about death and its implications. He had watched his mother die in bed from a particularly bad outbreak of smallpox, caught from a woman whose condition had escaped the attentions of the nurses at Ellis Island by sheer misfortune.

His family had been allocated a rat-infested slum tenement on Elisabeth Street, run by an unscrupulous Calabrian landlord, and they lived hand-to-mouth for the first year, living on the meagre pay his father brought home from his subway job as an electrician. When he had died, Harley was a bare five years old, petite and weak as a kitten, no match for the rougher Italian kids of similar age who commanded the neighborhood street corners, sitting imperiously on their stoops like miniaturised versions of the 'men of respect' they imitated. Many years later, in his late teens, Harley – a thin, rakish Jew – would work with these boys, masterminding robberies and running numbers between policy banks around the city. But in the meantime, to them, he was fair game if he stepped across the boundary of another neighborhood. He knew that these areas were clearly delineated, and to trespass was to encourage a severe beating from these mini-mobsters.

Harley sat on the roof overlooking the Junkyard Taverna, waiting for a drunk to roll. He was hungry, not having eaten enough in the last two days, and it was time he made a move.

He waited and his opportunity arose. A tall man, middle-aged and staggering, made his way into the sunlight, struggling for his watch chain. Harley jumped onto the fire escape, hurtling down the steps, and slid down the sliding ladder to the alleyway beneath. He couldn't believe his good fortune. The drunk was passed out, lying on a pile of stinking refuse bags, his arm draped over his chest. He reached out to the drunk's pocket and removed his bulging pocketbook, rifling through its contents.

*It never rains, but it pours,* he thought. He walked towards the street, happier than he had been in months. He felt a strong vice-like grip on his shoulder, and he spun around. The drunk had woken up, demanding the return of his wallet. In a jolt of fear, Harley's foot had struck out hard in escape, catching the man squarely in the throat. He dropped Harley, grabbing his throat, his face turning purple as he struggled for air. Instead of running as he should have, Harley was rendered immobile, capable of only watching the man as he collapsed to the ground.

Harley found his feet, and ran, bells ringing in the distance, increasing as they grew closer. If they nailed him, he would be taken straight to Juvenile Hall. There, he knew, he would not make it out. He was still far too green around the gills for that. He found an open doorway, and slid inside. It was an old warehouse, filled with junk and a scattering of broken hypodermic needle plungers. He guessed that he had found an old opium den that had been vacated due to seemingly endless police raids. The "Chinks" were the main port of call if you wanted that shit. He had been told that by his Uncle Eli before the old fart had died from emphysema a year later. An old fart with fascinating stories about the city he grew up in, and loved like a mother. The city that never sleeps. You could still open your window at night and experience New York without even going out there. Fights, shootings, and every form of communication it had to offer the average out-of-towner. Harley had borne aural witness one night, when he was three years old, to what he had learned later to be a particularly nasty alleyway rape. The echoes of her petrified

48

screams had never left him, reverberating in his memory ever since. It had made the front page of every newspaper in the city the following day, and a massive manhunt had been initiated by the cops. Try as they did, as diligent as they had been, they failed to find the perps, and put it down to someone from out of state, filing it instead.

Night had fallen upon him before he ventured outside again, taking great pains to remain undetected. He looked around and was satisfied that he was alone. A massive rat ambled languorously past him, brushing his ankle and made him jump. The city was alive, as usual, with the anguished car horns blasting the asshole in front to "get da fuck outta dere!" and the occasional distant burst of a machine gun (it would be a couple of years yet before Thompson patented the much vaunted 'Tommy Gun,' the weapon of choice of hoods everywhere when the Volstead Act was passed, and the lawless anarchy of prohibition engulfed the city, just as it would several others). He made his way to Times Square, passing through darkened alleys and dead side streets, the sound of the hustle and bustle getting ever closer. It was tourist season and the night was a veritable smorgasbord of pilfering potential. A boy could get rich from the lush pickings which the darkness brought, like well-heeled rats scavenging the remains of a street fair. A feast for the impoverished, to say the least!

Harley stood in the shadows of Times Square watching the degradation play out like a scene from one of those silent newfangled cinematograph films, but with sound so terrifying that he cowered there, afraid to step into the fray. He spotted a well-to-do couple walking towards him. They would do for openers, he thought. A nice easy starter to the main course he contemplated. He followed behind them at twenty feet until they reached the subway steps.

*Crap-ola!*

He dared not to down there but, Christ, he was hungry. There was little choice in it for him. If he made a move, it would have to be now. If they went down there, they were dead as Lincoln, anyway. It was then that he had the flash. He would spare them that fate, robbing them in the process.

He ran the twenty feet, calling out to them. They turned to see his dirty face peering at them, looking on in naïve amusement as he outlined their fate.

'Pleeease, mister. Don't go down there at night. It ain't safe. Get a taxicab for your wife's sake. *Please!*'

The man, a little older than his father when he died, looked down and patted caressed his face gently (to the obvious disgust of his wife who thought it beneath him), grateful for the boy's concern. The time had come. Harley's eyes darted over him, scanning for an opening. The man, kneeling now, hugged him and Harley's hand slowly entered the inner sanctum of the man's coat, extracting the thick, black leather wallet, placing it in his own coat. The man stood up and reached into his coat. Harley's eyes widened as he swallowed hard.

*He's gonna see it ain't there.*

The man reached into the opposite pocket, taking out some pocket change, handed it to the boy, his eyes tearful.

'Thank you, sonny. You be going on your way, now. It's very late,' he said, before walking to the sidewalk, hailing a taxi. Harley nodded, and walked off, slowly graduating to a full sprint, thanking God for small mercies. The old guy looked rich, based on his attire and finery. He would be set up for a long time, he thought. Not that *that* would stop him. It was almost a recreational sport in this day and age – habitual with a seductive quality he could not articulate due to his youth.

He walked into an alleyway leading to the base of the Brooklyn Bridge, finally opening the wallet. As imagined, it was filled with small bills – tens and twenties – and his heart jumped. For the first time in his life, he felt an overwhelming rush of guilt, shame and regret. He hadn't ever cared about his victims, not once. But that man – the man who had shown such kindness to him, although under the disapproving glare of his wife – his unwitting benefactor – had shown more warmth to him than virtually any other of his kind ever had – or likely ever would again.

*Well*, he thought, *those are the breaks!*

He counted as he walked aimlessly. He was out of danger, now. A tin can rattled off a doorway and his head shot up to meet the sound, his eyes darting left and right. He was not alone, after all.

'Well, lookit what we got ovah here! Shouldn't you be in bed at this hour, kid? Whatcha doin' out heah?'

He was being surrounded by a *borgata (street gang)* of four tough, well-abled boys, boys who would be glad to take his 'newfound life' if it took a beating to get it from him.

'What's that you got 'dere? You got somethin' you wanna show me, kid?' the tall one asked, his eyes scanning Harley's with a schizophrenic-like death stare. They were backing him into the wall of MacGovern's Tavern, blocking any chance of escape.

*Run*, he told himself.

But he couldn't. There was no way out. He was hemmed in far too tightly.

The tall one delivered an unseen blow to his cheek that smarted, making his eyes water and his nose tingle with the impact. Shaking, Harley knew it was now or never. He fought like a thing possessed, but was slammed hard against the wall again, knocking him out cold.

The last thing he heard was their uproarious laughter and the sound of a police whistle as they scattered towards the bridge underpass.

Harley awoke to the passing overhead lights of a hospital corridor as a gurney wheeled him to a bed – and back to destitution. The man who was, at first, so kind to him would finger him for the robbery in a line-up; the older boys who had ambushed him were about five hundred bucks richer; and he, Harley Leitman, would sit for a few years in a rathole Juvie center, before being released into the depths of abject poverty once again.

*The motto of this story,* he said to himself, *is never count your chickens before they hatch.*

The next time, he would remember.

If there *was* one.

**THE END**

# Untitled

By Bransha Gautier

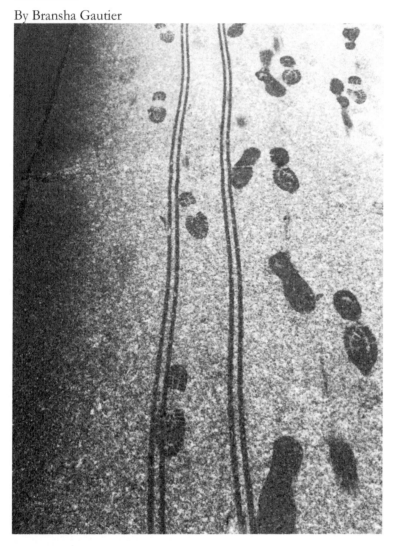

# Playing at Being Poets

By David Subacchi

We thought we'd seen him off
But he poked a finger
Into our eyes,
His erratic snow flakes
Straining to fall,
Blown here and there
By an inconsistent wind.

But although premature
She threw back
Her cloudy covering,
Allowing sunlight
To enter between the cracks,
Challenging his determination,
Warming our resistance.

In the town centre
We huddle in our usual
Hiding places,
Eat bread, drink
Wine from Portugal
And strong coffee,
Play at being poets.

# Morning on the Llanos

By Lorraine Caputo

The broad-canopy trees     the lakes
    of the morning *llanos*
       are full of birds
          all color, all sizes
*Babos* awaken     & colonies
    of capybaras congregate
       on the sandy shores
Anteaters jog across the plain
    shaggy fur bouncing
The night's rain
    shimmers in droplets
         on blades of grass
Doors open of
    wattle & daub homes
       tin-roofed     often windowless
Near one     small children gather
    the brush their bare-
       backed father machetes

# Frustrated Crab

By Jan Ball

You are in another *finishing academic paper*
*mode* when I want to use the computer
to choose theater dates at the Asolo
Theater in Sarasota, Florida for The Crucible.

I read Stacy Schiff's The Witches of Salem
two years ago so understand Miller's comparison
of those hysterical adolescents with the witch hunt
McCarthy Trials even though the original was
three hundred years ago and the Trials
within my lifetime.

I hurricane out of the study and fume
at the kitchen table like a moody teen-ager
after banging the dishes from the dishwasher
for emphasis as I ram them into the Florida
cupboard while I hear you hunt and peck
to find those last perfect phrases
on the computer keys.

Finally, your wool-lined slippers shuffle along
the marble tiles of our sub-tropical condo;
then you are next to me, kissing my shoulder,
a self-described *frustrated crab*.

We return to the computer together,
minimize your academic work, and find
the best date left for snowbirds at the Asolo,
preferably on the aisle, at least for one of us.

# Untitled

By Sohini Shabnam

# Failed Moon Poem

By William Barker

Enough similes
to choke upon,

to easily (dis)honor
the subject,

shredded for privacy,
mixed into cement,

and poured between molds,
for mass production.

The lens of God's spyglass,
a consummate pearl

upon a backdrop of diamonds,
a ghostly face,

a shard of glass
upon black velvet...

We've heard them all,
dreamed them all,

planted many a metaphor,
watched them grow,

before hacking them to bits,
seems to be a requirement

to get membership
into the club.

Thin overtures,
too numerous to count,

blaring, cluttering,
proclaiming adoration

to our own Lady Chameleon,
perched there

among a jeweled river,
reflected upon the night sea

sewn with abounding stanzas,
making even an attempt

with any originality,
cumbersome.

I don't write poetry
at night anymore,

so the sun keeps
stealing all the glory,

which is fine,
because poets

praise the sun too little,
God, booze, cats, and the moon

too much, leaving good old Sol
deserving of some wine,

chocolate-covered strawberries,
and romance, if you ask me.

# The Balancing Act

By John Gray

Meat in the oven
seems more urgent
than the disorganized desk
your hands muddle through.

What is the meal for tonight to be?
Why are your family as prickly as porcupines?
Gossip goes on around you,
twisting words and glances.
Here you are merely criticized.
At home, it takes constant effort
to keep your head high.

Your boss asks will the report be
finished on time.
Days are unpredictable.
You never know
when managing your life will be called on.

# Instagram

By Karol Nielsen

I joined Instagram to promote my upcoming book, but it soon became a place to share artistic images of mosaics, architectural details, mountains, spring flowers, and poems. I collected over 1,000 followers. Some congratulated me when my book came out but hundreds endorsed my artistic photos, including a sketch from a time before writing took over as my way to express myself. I followed poets but quickly I was drawn to the minimalist subculture that turns cropped angles of buildings into art. I developed crushes on strangers, and was devastated when a young hipster said he stopped posting a year ago after his accident. What accident? He didn't say. He posted selfies in a stack and when I flipped through I saw his prosthetic leg. I didn't know what to say to this stranger who had suffered like this. I follow a woman who lost 300 pounds and underwent surgery to remove her loose skin. She is upbeat and inspiring even when haters trash her for gaining back some weight. I follow some celebrities, too, like the cast of a teen television series I binge watch over and over. It feels frivolous, a guilty pleasure like Boston Cream donuts. Then one of the actors from the show posted wise words from O. Henry: "Write what you like; there is no other rule."

# Untitled

By Bransha Gautier

# Gloria's Cousin

By Jan Ball

Henry and I suggest Boka
for dinner when Gloria comes
to town. She brings her cousin,
Marjorie, who is a curator
at Chicago's Contemporary
Art Museum and lives
just a few blocks from us.
Marjorie tells us about recent
Exhibitions like *Otobong Nkanga:*
*To Dig a Hole That Collapses,*
and Gloria talks about the slots
in Las Vegas.

We are enjoying our *steak frites*
with garlic spinach when Henry
starts wheezing. His eyes get red,
and his speech becomes nasal and
hard to understand. *What's wrong?*
I ask from across the table, concerned.
He croaks: *I don't know. It's like I get*
*when I'm around cats.* Gloria's cousin,
sitting next to Henry, blushes

from her chin to her blonde eyebrows.
*I have a Persian cat,* she explains
like apologizing for double-booking
an important appointment.

Henry and I pay our portion of the bill
and scurry into the fresh air for our
Uber as if we're escaping the butcher's
wife. The following Wednesday, I text
Gloria in Vegas, *When are we going
to see your cousin again?* She replies,
*Never, she's too embarrassed.*

A few months later, I see Marjorie
on the 155 bus. We both pretend
we don't know each other.

# Serving

By John Grey

The couple at table five
are starting to grow restless
and the diner at seven
is unhappy with how his
meal's been cooked.
Eight's been waiting twenty minutes
for the beer he ordered.
Three is complaining
because there's no kid's meals
on the menu.

People have a rare opportunity
to not be demanding of themselves.
Instead, they expect
the impossible from you.
All you can do is smile and say,
"I'll be with you in a minute."

You are at the behest
of everyone's newly acquired self-importance.
It's a bitter-sweet setup
for what tips may follow.

# Christmas Eve

By Rp Verlaine

I say nothing
as the sirens
and flashing lights
pass in the briefest of blurs.

Later I'll reason
It happened too fast
and both of us were
contempt of court wrong.

But my heart
reached out to
shivering kid a hundred
windbreakers couldn't thaw.

Hiding in terror
behind a mailbox
in swirling snow from police
hugging a woman's purse.

## Do You Know

By Mark A. Fisher

the ghost in the hibiscus that sways
back and forth in crimson waves
like cycles of a dream
when in life she'd stand and pluck
a single blossom for her hair
then turn to smile becomingly
and laugh at me
never knowing
I'd be waiting every evening
for her smile never fading
near the hibiscus
that still is swaying

## Colossus
By William Barker


Fifty years
since gas stole
your last breath,

sealing you away
in the kitchens
of Death
without cold milk,

soul departing
like saw blades flying,
scarring the cheeks
of two innocent cherubs,
imprinting them forever
with your fast shadow.

You threaded
the noose,
leaving it on
sweet Nicholas' pillow.

Frieda whispered

to the ghost

at your typewriter,

plumping in that silence

like a croissant,

until her fourteenth

year when truth

imploded Dad's secret—


*Suicide,*

gutting a dolls innocence

and the muse soon knocking,

splashing the sun

upon canvas

while she worked

furiously

with the moon

in her eyes.

# Catfish

By Lee Ellis

Snagged in cotton and linen surf, my body drifts,
   denied the oxygen of your kiss.
Craving your autumn hands
   on my skin of scoured sand,
   balm of want with the hint of reprobation,
   wounds emerging as broken shells in a cold wind.
This hermit heart, trying on new homes for
   good fit, beats foolish in its exposure.
You pull at my flotsam hope until it sinks, settles, sloughs
   dead dreams into the current rush.
Recalling your voice of oil and obsidian "I can't. I won't." in
my ear,
   against my neck, against my desperation,
      against, "You must."
The pinch of vinegar and lime
   in my jaw as your hips heated mine
as your blood-sea struck my shore
   the core
       of your hunger, a shark at bay
   your pulse raw, banging,
   "I.      Should.      Go."
Go, then.
      Stay.
Your face here, over me
   apparition
   made flesh in
      my tidal need.

## Sedative

By Lee Ellis

Here again is 4 am.

Here again the shivering apart

      and the tiny yellow moon that promises sleep

            until dawn.


Here

      more thoughts of you

      more fury

      more cavernous despair.


Give me the little moon on my tongue

      and cold stars over crashing

            waves

            goodbye.

# The Mechanic
By Neal Amandus Gellaco

I was permitted to remain a tenant under Joseph
Gilbert despite my inability to pay rent in exchange for my
mechanical services in repairing some faulty gears in his car
and realigning various electrical fixtures around his mansion. I
supposed too that Joseph allowed this lapse in payment,
contrary to his character, since I had once readily lent him
twenty thousand in cash to save his once failing business.
From then on, he had a warmer attitude toward our
friendship, I should say, and a more disciplined handling of
his monetary affairs. The wheel of fortune had rotated in
those two years, and Joseph, now prosperous and with
flourishing investments, was to repay his debts to me, who
now latched onto him in financial dependency.

His monstrous wife disapproved of the transaction, as
much as I disapproved of her. I took pleasure in gloating at
her distorted, warty face whenever we met on the hallways,
and she did nothing but huff, all because her husband—my
personal acquaintance before her lover, she should
remember—sided in my favor and not hers. Kick him out,
she said, but here I still was staying on.

Mary Wilbur was the female doppelganger of my
father, and I can think of no greater insult to both. She was
adamant on controlling all of Joseph's actions (except one, it
turned out) as much as Father controlled mine in my
childhood, but Joseph was now advantageous—I was *not* in
my childhood—to have his own courage and agency to
retaliate and stand his ground—I did not. The sole cause I
had to despise Father more than Mary Wilbur was that he had
plagued me for a longer time: twenty-five years from my birth

until his recent death by fire—his car exploded with him in it. I felt no remorse since he deserved such a punishment: for my desultory childhood when he locked me up in the basement; my despairful adolescence when he allowed me no friends and no time outside of home except school; and my decrepit adulthood when he spent every money in my account as though he owned it.

Should I be cursed to reside with the wench Mary Wilbur for the next twenty-five years, I may grow to despise her more severely than I did Father, but I doubt Joseph will want to keep her by his side for long. The thought of an impending divorce gave me my peace of mind, remaining my third source of solace, other than Joseph Gilbert's face and figure and my thesis to be published in the International Journal of Theoretical Physics. I had retreated from the library, after some revisions on the latter's foundational theoretical frame, when I met the wench Mary Wilbur on the second-floor hallway. I was both elated and saddened when she informed me that, "My husband and I will go away tomorrow to a lake house for the weekend."

Why hadn't Joseph spoken to me himself? But that was no matter—if they were to leave, at least I was to be spared the view of *her* face for a day. There was a tense pause in the dimmed hallway, for I did not know what she expected me to say in response. I made to check the wires of the defunct light fixtures, which I was supposed to mend as soon as I could (my services *were* required in exchange for bed and board).

"In our absence, you may have visitors over, but I doubt you'll have any, now that your Father is dead."

Her remark didn't unnerve me, but her tone hoped it would. I long accepted the fact that I have no use for friends and never had the talent for acquiring any. The closest I came to one, was in my personal acquaintanceship with Joseph Gilbert which I daresay *might* burst into friendship very soon. The wench wobbled away, and I finished my job completely before night fell. The mended lights in the hallway proved to be brighter than Mary Wilbur's head or face will ever be.

That evening before their departure, I overheard their conversation through the thin, wooden walls—I always did listen to their talks—since their bedroom was adjacent to mine. Their talks were never anything substantial—how could it be so, if one were conversing with the wench Mary Wilbur? I listened because Joseph's deep voice soothes my nerves and readies me for sleep as though he were right beside me reciting a lullaby.

"This is the last night we are disturbed by that pesky Albert Weed."

It was the wench speaking, and I sat up on my bed wide awake.

"Truly, my darling, if we could only pluck him out when we do not want him around, all the better. We must leave as early as possible tomorrow."

It was the wench's husband. The nerve of people to hit you on the back with black ingratitude. I clenched my fists, gripping the linen sheets covering my bed. They must suffer, I thought, they were no better than my father. *She* was no surprise, but *he* was a punch to the gut by an unsuspecting blow. There was a pounding against my chest as I snuck into the garage where I had repaired his car earlier. Its screws were easy to undo as it had been for me to fix—I was no amateur in dooming vehicles to fail; I have done so once before. I hoped to be cunning and loosened the gears only so slightly that I foresaw the car, carrying the ingrate and his wench, lethargically unravel as they drove from the house until it exploded in the middle of the street—a crime untraceable and unattributable to me. I went to sleep satisfied.

I awoke earlier that my norm to retighten the screws. With a rested mind, I wished to undo all of last night's caprice. Though their offense deserved the punishment, Joseph was too handsome to die, and his death would be a waste—and on principle, I try not to get involved in wasteful deaths. Materially as well, if he were to die, where then was I to go? I, Albert Weed, was a man noble in thought and, in undoing the act, remained noble in deed.

Entering the garage, I found it empty, and out on the road, there was nothing in sight. I sighed: it would be a terrible inconvenience to look for another tenancy, and the new landlord may not be as beautiful as Joseph Gilbert was. I had no other course of action as of the moment but to take my breakfast and read the daily paper and wonder if the explosion and their deaths would be enough of a spectacle to merit tomorrow's headline.

A note on the table was underneath the cutlery, and it relayed that Joseph and Mary left before sunrise to catch their train and that they would deposit the car in the station parking lot.

I was relieved. I had not known their exact destination, but the distance to the station was insufficient for the full unraveling of screws I had plotted: I could simply retighten the screws sometime between now and their arrival back. I smiled at my coffee, paced my unknowingly agitated breaths, and came to my desk on the second floor to work on my thesis until lunchtime.

Halfway through my grilled chicken breast, I heard the phone ring. A female voice inquired whether this was the residence of Mr and Mrs Joseph Gilbert, and I said yes. She then asked if I was family, and I also said yes.

"Sir, we regret to inform you of the most unfortunate circumstance: the ten o'clock train derailed and crashed onto the platforms, and around a hundred people, including Mr Joseph Gilbert and Mrs Mary Wilbur-Gilbert, were crushed and killed. The cause we could be sure of as of now is a mechanical error."

She gave her condolences, and asked if I were available to retrieve their salvageable belongings and the car later in the day when they would be sent to the station where they departed from. I said I would retrieve their belongings, put down the phone, and did not know what to think. My mind went blank. I felt something crack, much how I imagined the train crushed the platform's pavement and the hundreds of bystanders' bones.

I alighted from a cab and strode toward the train station where I saw Joseph's suitcase, thrashed and splintered, beside the *hers* which were even more beaten and destroyed than his, among a few others. I left hers with the superintendent to donate to charity; and this noble decision helped more people in the long run—clothes and accessories went to the poor, and I had only one heavy suitcase to carry instead of three. It was also the superintendent who handed me the car keys from the depository, and with a deep voice he repeated his condolences, "What a tragedy," to which I only half agreed.

I walked to the car and sat inside; the interior smelled of the soap and the cologne Joseph used. Inside the compartment were the wench's gloves, which she had misplaced, no doubt due to her innate incompetence. I tossed the gloves out the window in mock celebration of her death, and I watched it mingle with the dirt where it belonged. I opened one of Joseph's cases, brushed my hand against the soft fabrics of his clothes, took his suede outdoor jacket, and wore it in triumph. With the ignition started and the engine revving, I drove back to the mansion with the disappointment of never seeing Joseph again, to be content with merely smelling and touching and feeling the remnants he left behind. Outside the car window, the sun was at its orange peak, half hidden in the clouds, as though it too was joining me in my semi-triumph. The day was bright; the air was light. I kept the collar of the coat around my nose, like a scarf, and each inhale was liberating. With each breath, I had one less problem and no more anxieties. This was the life I deserved, unburdened by debts and high on the drug of mixed sweat, soap, and cologne—a life I acquired after a quarter of a century of living. His scent was fading when I heard the telltale clink; the resulting bang a moment later was deafening. I was left with no time to ponder if hell did exist, and if it did, would it be this hot for eternity, and if it were, will I be cursed to see the wench and Father once again.

# Fire Dancing

By William Barker

Mom had a bounce
in her step preparing dinner
on the old range; oven smoking
above bubbling pots; no werewolf
eyes on Dad despite the moon's
shine, cascading.

These aberrant evenings
when belligerence and chaos
sneak out the back door
to smoke cigarettes in nearby
woods, feeling unwelcome for once,
behind the cracking
white plaster.

Mom at the stereo,
the flat clop of plastic
tape cassettes being scoured,
soon the tunes blaring—
bubble gum fifties, mystic
sixties; clapping,
singing ensuing.

Into the living room,
dancing like daisies
in the wind,
these rare nights
along the rainbow's end,
my beautiful Mother
on young legs,
smiling as if cradling
her firstborn again.

The weights and pressures
of the world, irrelevant,
alcoholism, a dry desert,
lost in the revelry of music
forged from the finest
feelings, memories, and energies.

My Father, whiskey in hand,
watching her from the couch,
as if realizing love and attraction
for the first time again.

The glorious music
of their youth raging in defiance
of another average evening's
melancholia,
with television trays
and nightly news.

My Mother's infectious sensuality
ultimately pulled my Father
from his grumpy log kingdom,
now on his feet,
the marigold carpet
of the living room,
a dance floor aflame.

I even joined in,
playing tissue box drums
or air-guitar
like a wild fool.

For the duration
of a few songs
our family
wasn't a whisper
among neighbors,

and a terrible cliché.

No screaming.
No fighting.
Only revelry.

For the children of an alcoholic,
nothing much survives
besides chaos
and lost time.

It is nice to smell rain
after the storm,
and forget the storm.

To fall back upon that soft
magic, before the feather
of reality is grounded.

These are the fondest
pearly evenings,
stretching forever through time
like a long country road
in Autumn.

# At the Abbey

By David Subacchi

My leather shoes
Weigh heavily
On old stone floors
But younger feet
Rubber shod
Move more gently
Across memorials
To poets and generals.

Amongst ring tones
And recorded guides
I am silently in awe
Allowed to enter
For no charge to worship
But asked not to stray
Beyond allocated seats.

My soft shoed friends
Who paid for admission
Zig zag before altars
Flashing cameras
Their excited activity
Gradually overwhelmed
By the abbey's grandeur.

Later a cassocked figure
Approaches slowly
Smiling understandingly
And I wonder whether
The dark robe might conceal
A machine gun.

# Ser 1

By Carmen Caro

# Deconstruction

By Allison Whittenberg


In the name of the Father, the Son, and the ... oh,
you know the rest....

I'm Sister Ardeth Margaret Katherine D'Arby, and I
have just been sentenced to three years. He knows what He's
doing. It will be three years well spent, that I assure you.
Those souls locked away need my guidance, and it won't be
my first time on the inside, as they say. It won't be so bad. I
hope we will be able to stay together though. The others
Sisters Jacqueline and Carol. I pray that they won't split us up.
I've known them since I first entered the order. We were so
young then, thinking we could save the world.

The judge had such harsh words for us. Such words.
He said we were "dangerously irresponsible." To that Sister
Carol said, "Nuclear warfare is dangerously irresponsible!"
And that Judge told her to Shut Up. Shut up, he said. Imagine
such talk. Shut up, he said.

Some government property should be destroyed. All
the papers made such a big deal about you the blood. We
used our blood to make crosses on the missiles. I've been
with the order for 20 years. I would do it again. And then we
used a hammer. Pounding and pounding . If only we could
turn it into salt.

# A letter to Tali /Tali Cohen Shabtai

By Tali Cohen Shabtai,

There's a whole world
waiting for you
around the darker
corner of life

in which
you are adept enough to sort clothes
of the same
ethnic group of
the black cloth
of your life.

If you hadn't been a little better
than the decorations that would add
figurativeness

so as to decorate the rhetoric
of the black cloth of your life

I promise you that you would
get
to see
a star fall in the dark!

# Grandpa's Tattoos
By Jan Ball

are not the psychedelic swirls
and orange whorls like we see
on our parents' bodies,
even a topless Hawaiian woman
on Dad's forearm that he can make
hula when he tightens his muscles,

and not the "of course" printed
indelibly as twin tattoos on Auntie's
and Dad's torsos to commemorate
what Dad said to the interventionist
when he asked, "Will you  agree to go
to rehab," and Dad replied, "of course".

Instead, they tell us that Grandpa's
tattoos are just a dot in three places:
the base of his abdomen, in front,
and one miniscule blue dot on each hip
to indicate where the technician
should point the radiation for Grandpa's
prostate cancer.

# Dens of our Grandfathers

By Stephen Finlay

Holy colors -- deep autumn orange and yellows and reds. I can imagine strapping a crown of twigs to my head, and a mask for my face, and dancing the round dances through fields pregnant with corn and soybeans, until I collapse roadside in spent, orgasmic satiation. A dance of submission, of humble, beseeching desperation in this insulating and forgotten tract of Illinois. A place no one travelled unless it was home, or else accidentally. And then to make these offerings. To hang a deer from its back legs, to open its throat, to quench the thirst of the gods in the grass. To return a stillborn child to the soft earth by the new moon. To return to work in the hammer factory or the field on Monday, while heaving Gaia breathes into life the dawn's fog, the distant deer on the frost-flecked grass, the steam of the Casey's breakfast pizza, the colors of our grandparents' dens. So dark, that blood-black wood.

# Paisley: Once Upon A Time

By Linda Imbler

Bright shirts with hippie pantaloons,
Persian pickles, printed swirls,
Sixties music, signature tunes,
Playing on lazy afternoons,
Tie-dyed ornamental whirls.

Printed jackets, so Nehru necked,
Music scene these teens took part in,
Patterned paisley where forms connect,
Woven shawls worn for best effect,
Their quest for peace unshaken.

# Grave People

By Rameez Ahmad Bhat

Exhausted by his long walk, his mind settled on the idea of taking a rest at a place his eyes caught sight of to the right of his not far from where he was. "Ah, a farm", he exclaimed in a tone of satisfaction. He paced his steps towards it, reaching there in a couple of moments. As he moved toward the edge of what he had thought as a farm, however, what his sight touched upon was that it a long stretch of land under the shadows of trees flushed with greenery. In the middle of the land, he saw a large chinar tree overlooking the small stretch of land to the left of it. He rushed to the chinar tree to rest for a little. As soon as he reached it, what he saw to his amazement was that he found himself the only person among the dead, prompting him raise his hands and say fatiha for their souls. No sooner had he uttered "asalamualiekum ya" than a wailing voice of a woman hit his ears. He stopped. Turned around. Saw a woman wailing in front of a grave. Not saying the fatiha, he quickened towards and asked her, "Hum shera, che kyaxi wadan"? (Sister why are you crying?). Sensing a voice behind her, the woman wiped off her tears, stopped crying, grabbed her bag, got up on her feet, turned around, looked him in the eye and replied, "Yi chu meon posh" (This is my son). "When did he die?" he inquired. Sighing a long and deep breath, "Next month it will be twenty years" she stopped and then continued, "I can't foget that day. He had gone to a shop for milk and snacks for our guests...my brother...his mamu...gone for milk he was sent with blood-drenched body. It was his 20th Rohan posh today. I have been here praying to Allah for his return ever since. I have been to every shrine but of no avail. My prayers do not even go beyond my rooftop let alone reaching the sky. I want him back in my life because for I am alone... I had only son everything in this world. Now that he is no more here ... I feel and am devastated."He listened with utter and serene attention to her and seeing her falling into dead silence, he asked her to give him eleven loaves of bread to pray for her son. "I have tried this for years now. It even does not work now. Times have changed," she retorted quickly. Again raising his hands in prayer, his lips quiver. No sooner had he finished this than a creaking sound from the grave of Intizar Ahmad. She looked around and found to her amazement people rising from the graves, heading towards the village. Shocked at what she saw was happening, "moaji" (mother) hit her ears. She recognized the voice at once, turned around and found her son in the clothes he had gone that day to the market. "How did you know I was your mother?" "How could I forget the only face moaji"? She embraced him as tight as she could. As soon as she turned around to thank the man who had prayed for her son, he was no more to see. She was sad she could not say her thanks to the man and his prayers. The mother and her son headed towards the village, his index finger in her hand like twenty years ago when she would take him to the *urs* next village. It took them so long to reach home for the only path to the village was full of the grave people walking home. Everything except for his home had changed. It was a happiness to revisit him home to cherish. As he set his foot inside, Fatima woke up to the voice of Intizar, "moaji, moaji, crackdown chu nebir kin" (Mother, mother, outside is crackdown).

# Asmodeus

By Swarnav Misra

Why do you behold me the way you do?
Those eyes, lifeless as such
Grim Reaper's scythe shall shy away
Is it not sinful to snivel the sinistral eye
Whilst I paint the Raven blue?
I can renounce the Gospel of Mammon
I can abandon my Garden of Eden
Yet, you seek the Asmodeus in me
And so I make you my Lilith.

Come now, defy all hurdles,
Resist all restraint
Let us give this dying world
The chaos it's craving
The doom it deserves
Let the bluebird fly away
Let the drops dry away
Let it rain blood and tears
And even as you consume
My hundredth heir
Gambling Tellus' fate,
Nine Hell shall descend as we mate.

# Untitled

By Derek Roper

# Notices of Death

By John Grey

Ray overdosed on sleeping pills.
Joe was found in his bath,
wrists slit.
Don touched a live wire.
Rita smashed head on into a truck.

And then there were the long, slow, surrenders:
Amy to cancer,
Dave to multiple sclerosis.

I read the death notices,
over coffee, in the morning.
If there are life notices,
then I've yet to find them.

# The Shadowed Sky

By Catherine Alexander

(First Published in Margins Magazine, University of Toronto. Scarborough September 10, 2020)

In a Venezuelan farmhouse made of stone and wood, Elena skips into the kitchen in a nightie sewn by her mother. The lace on the gown's collar and pocket all embroidered by Abuelita, her grandmother.

Black beans and rice on the wood stove in a country kitchen. The fridge runs when power does.

The big house and farm go back more generations than Abuelita can count. Now there is just one milk cow, Pepita. Tomatoes in the garden, chickens in coops. A mango tree near the barn.

Through the kitchen window, Elena spies pigeons on the portico railing. Later she might be allowed to throw out bits of *arepa*, corn flat bread.

"Mami and Papi working?"

"Manuel and Blanca are teaching in the village as usual," says her grandmother. "How about some breakfast? Here's an orange. Shall I slice it the way you love?"

"Yes please, Abuelita." Elena bites off the fruit from each slice. Abuelita takes the peelings and creates letters on the table: C-O-O. "See," she says, "these spell what the pigeons sing. Do you hear them?"

"I hear, I hear! Can I go and watch them on the portico?"

"Don't you want breakfast?"

"Not now, Abuelita. I want to see the pigeons first."

"Okay, but no further than the portico. I'll watch you from the window."

Elena slips arepa bits into her nightie's pocket and leaps out of her chair.

"Wait!" says Abuelita. "Give them these rinds, too."

As soon as Elena opens the door, the pigeons scatter. "Wait birdies," she cries, opening her palm to reveal arepa bits and orange rinds.

"Just be still," Abuelita says. "They'll be back."

Elena stands like one of the soldiers she's seen in the city square, looking at him from the bus window.

Soon a few birds strut down the railing, bobbing their heads. Elena lets treats drop from her hand. The rush of plumage begins. "That's all," says Elena, as she closes the door.

After her favorite breakfast of rice with butter and cream, Elena wears an embroidered blouse and gathered skirt while she plays on the floor. "Coo-coo," she says to her dollies. "That's what the pigeons sing."

Abuelita says, "You know, Elena, pigeons are really doves."

"Doves?"

"Yes, love birds. White doves are a symbol of peace and love."

Abuelita takes out her quartro, a small guitar with four strings, and begins to play a love song.

"Does Mami love Papi?" asks Elena.

"Of course. That's why they had you."

Abuelita's face has deep, intertwined lines, her flesh is growing loose, but her smile brings buoyancy to Elena. "What will we do today?" Elena asks.

"First I must milk Pepita," says Abuelita. "You stay here."

When she's finished, Abuelita carries a half-bucket of milk, sets it on the portico, and enters the house.

"Now we can play if the rains hold off. It's the stormy season," she tells Elena. She hands her a cotton bag of seeds for the birds. They head to the garden to settle under the ficus.

Birds with orange breasts skitter close. "Elena," says Abuelita. "Those are turpials, the birds of our country. Remember I told you?"

"Yes, Abuelita." says Elena, as she throws seeds. Soon yellow-breasted orioles join the scramble.

"And see, *mi querida*, here comes a dusty white dove wanting his fill. Today we are graced. Let me play a folk tune about their cooing."

Elena looks up. "But there's a shadow in the sky."

"That's a cloud, Elena. A big one. Feel the wind. *Dios mio*! A storm is approaching."

"But I want Mami and Papi to come home before it starts!"

"You must rush inside, little one. I'll put the cow in the barn."

Elena takes off to the farmhouse. She can barely close the door against the wind. Hailstones clatter on the old roof. Lightning flashes across the sky while trees crash the portico.

Elena runs to every window. "Abuelita! Abuelita!"

Electricity sparks; the house goes dark. Elena sobs, holding two dollies. "Abuelita!"

Finally, her grandmother crashes in the door, blown forward by the gale. She throws off her wet clothes and grabs

Elena. "It will be all right, child; it will be all right. Let me start the fire and light the candles."

"I'm scared," screams Elena. "Mami and Papi will be washed away."

"That won't happen. They will be home soon. Don't worry, little one."

But Abuelita *is* worried. If the storm keeps up, the road from the village will flood. The only way home for her son and daughter-in-law is through the city, where armed guards attack protesters against the dictatorship. Billboard pictures of the president and his forces show what no villager wants to see.

Millions of people have fled the country because they have no food or supplies. No one dare complain to the government for fear of torture and death. Now with COVID, the situation has worsened. But the villagers, teachers and Abuelita know little of the pandemic.

"Elena, I'll make you *una taza de caliente,* all right?" Abuelita coaxes a smile from her *nieta.*

But not for long. As soon as Elena finishes her hot chocolate, she begins to sob. "I'm scared! What if my parents drown in the flood?"

"Come here, *mi presiosa.* Let me brush your hair. We don't even know if there's a flood. Your parents could be home any moment. The road may not be washed out."

"I want to go and find them, now!"

"Elena, we must stay here and be safe. The wind would blow you away."

Elena runs in circles while the wind blows against the stone walls, and inside the room, bringing a loud whoosh. The youngster shrieks. Abuelita distracts her by strumming the quarto. Soon Elena twirls and sings off key.

"You have rhythm in your feet that's missing in your voice," laughs Abuelita.

Elena grabs her doll in a whirling frenzy around the room.

Abuelita barely keeps up plucking her quarto. "Slow down, little love, or you'll fall down. You are getting too excited. Settle! Now, my dear, it's time for a rest. Play in your room while I clean up a bit."

After checking the fire, Abuelita paces back and forth on the only rug in the house, now trampled flat. She worries that Manuel and Blanca will take the road that runs by the square. She wrings her hands. Pulls at her grey hair. She's heard that armed guards have rifles aimed at protesters and passersby. She'd been afraid since Manuel and Blanca began teaching in the village. But if it weren't for them, village children wouldn't learn. Abuelita warned her son about dangers that floods present, leaving travelers no choice but the road to the city. And if the torrent continues, the old farmhouse could be in harm's way.

She hears Pepita mooing; she must have broken out of the barn. All Abuelita can do is pray that she will go back to safety. Winds are too strong for her to venture out.

∞

Putting the child to bed that night proves difficult. Elena tells her grandmother that guards with guns march on the square.

Abuelita's gaze widens. "How do you know that?"

"Mami and I went by on the old bus. I saw them."

"What? You saw them? When?"

"Christmas time."

"*Ay Dios Mio!*"

100

Hiding her fear, Abuelita helps Elena change into her nightie, slips the dolly in the child's arms. "You will be all right, mi querida, I am here with you."

Elena clasps her arms around her grandmother's neck. "Will my parents be home when I wake up in the morning?"

Abuelita whispers "God will make it so. She kisses the child and tucks her in.

∞

The night is long. Abuelita pulls out a bottle of rum from the cupboard, pours a glass half-full, and plops in her armchair with her rosary. After a while, she hears voices outside—

mutterings and the clamor of tumbling rocks. Portents of nature surrounding her farm, casting a spell. One refill of rum causes her to drop the beads and enter dreams of serpents and bird-eating tarantulas. Before sunrise she wakens clearheaded. More voices, deep and calling. She wrestles on her coat, hat and boots, ready to venture outside. Or so she thinks. After several workouts, she's blown back by the wind. Once inside, she still hears voices. She must go meet the forces. Using all her power and more, she makes another attempt and shoves the door open.

She tromps through muddy ravines and rotting tree trunks, while branches jab her arms and hail needles her face. No stars to help her navigate. Torrents slam her like a giant wave. In the distance, the barn has been sliced in half by a tree. Poor Pepita, where is she? And the mango tree? Abuelita presses both hands to her chest, fighting fear and exertion. Her movements slow and deliberate. What if she falls and careens down a ravine?

Floundering in the dark, she notices expanding shadows. What are these? Mysterious creatures haunting her? But their shapes resemble people—her people.

Through the mist, Manuel and Blanca stumble down the road, flanked by two villagers. Manuel leans forward, cradling his hand. Blanca holds one of his arms, a villager another.

"Madre!"

Abuelita hears the voice of her only son. He breaks through the line to reach his mother. "Manuel, mi hijo. What happened?"

"Just need a bandage."

"Let me see your hand."

"Not now."

"What happened?"

"Later," says Manuel.

Abuelita stifles her tears, trembling inside. "*Ay Dios mio*. Let's get you into the house and you can tell me more."

Then she sees Elena race from the house in her nightie.

"Elena!" cries Abuelita. "What are you doing out here? You'll get soaked and catch pneumonia!"

Blanca, drenched from the storm, dashes up to shield her daughter from the rainfall. Lifting her up, she says, "Here, my beautiful child, get under my coat."

"Is Papi hurt?" asks little Elena.

"Not to worry, darling. We'll fix his hand."

Once in the house, they peel off their wet clothes, piece by piece. Watery mud and silt falls on the floor. Abuelita rushes to revive the fire from the coals. The Venezuelan sun is just rising. She hears her chickens chatter. The rain stops.

"Madre!" says her son. "Let me tend the fire. You sit."

"Not until I see that hand."

"I already rinsed it. One soldier knifed me, but it's a clean cut and not bleeding. See?"

"I must wrap it properly."

"Mami, we need to take care of the villagers first."

"Of course, my son."

Abuelita and Manuel dress the villagers' cuts from knives and slashes from whips.

∞

"Now my son, tell me everything"

"Okay, Mami. I'll start from the beginning. We took the road to the city to check on you and Elena. Four fathers of our village students insisted on coming to protect us."

"How could they protect you?"

"They said they would cover us. I didn't think they could pull it off. But they did. Now two are missing."

"*Ay Dios.* Did they get shot?"

"I pray not. There were thousands of protestors and security forces in the square. I didn't know what was going on. Guards attacked with knives, whips, and rifles. And some National Guard vehicles ran into the crowd, killing anybody in their way."

"They are murderers!"

"Not only that. Police on motorcycles fired tear gas into the crowd. We could hardly breathe. Where Blanca and I huddled, the fathers of our students kept fighting back, despite tear gas and rifle shots. We started running, yelling for the villagers to join us. But they wouldn't. Finally, two caught up with us on the road home."

"*Gracias a Dios,*" says his mother.

103

In one bedroom, Blanca towels Elena's hair, and dresses her in warm clothes. The child begs for una taza de caliente. "Coming up," says Mami.

They all congregate around the table where Abuelita has set out the rice and beans. But no one seems to be hungry. Manuel, with his good hand, pokes in the cupboard for the rum bottle. "Mami, you been nipping?"

"There's another bottle behind it, son."

Manuel laughs and brings both bottles to the table.

He addresses the wounded villagers. "I worry about the other two? Were they behind you?"

"For a while, but they disappeared. We pray for their fast return. May God hear our prayers."

"Let's pray," says Manuel. Afterwards he lifts his glass. "Here's to the fathers who protected us. We owe you our lives!"

"No!" says a villager. "You teachers saved our children. They can now leave our poor village because they know letters, numbers, and more—unlike their parents. You and teacher Blanca son heroés! The other teachers always left because of little pay and crime in our village."

"You are too kind. Blanca and I are honored to be the village educators. May the blood on the road may someday be our leader's! Now let's rest for a while."

Villagers sleep on the floor. The family scatters in other rooms. Abuelita hears her cow. She races to the window, but no Pepita. She slips out the door and heads for the barn, half of it still standing. Inside, the two missing villagers are huddled around the cow.

She runs to them and gives Pepita a hug.

"Why did you not come to the house, amigos?"

"Okay here."

"No! You are hurt." She helps them up and on the path home, past the standing mango tree. The cow plods along for a while, then turns back to what's left of the barn.

Pigeons and orange-breasted turpials follow, watching the scene unfold.

Abuelita and the villagers trudge into the old farmhouse. The family is up and called to action. She collapses in her armchair.

"Es la voluntad de Dios, it's the will of God," says Abuelita, dribbling tears. "You all have escaped the regime forces. My precious Pepita will give us milk. I hear my chickens squawking in their coops. Even the mango tree still stands."

Manuel leaps up. "And I will rebuild the barn!"

Elena skips into the room in her nightie, completes a perfect *pirueta,* and climbs in Grandmother's lap.

Abuelita smoothes Elena's wispy brown hair. "How beautiful, my treasure. May you always be safe.

# Awareness

By F. Berna Uysal

# 2nd heartbreak

By F. Berna Uysal

# Crone

By F. Berna Uysal

# Coffee Mug Afternoon, 1986

By William Barker

### I.

I used to sniff the fresh grounds
in their soft pouch,
inhaling deeply the robust aromatics
of a new brew.

After Mom poured a cup, I'd watch
the swirling cream lighten the blackness,
imagining the glory of that first sip.

*"It looks like chocolate milk
without enough syrup." I mused.
"Can I try some, Mom?"*

*"Not until you're older,"*
she affirmed, *"end of story."*

### II.

One summer day,
home alone with my older brother,
I spied the glass carafe
brimming with soap suds in the sink,
but Mom's raspberry lipstick-stained mug,
still half-filled with coffee,
sitting upon the corn-colored Formica,
the last plumes of steam
gone hours ago.

I grabbed the mug,
set the microwave
to one minute,
and anxiously awaited
the best part of waking up.

To a seven-year-old boy
in the mid-eighties,
before everyone clutched a cup
out in the streets,
before coffee chains appeared
in every town and city,
this action felt dishonest,
almost like a betrayal,
the same way I'd feel
ten years later
drinking Dad's whiskey
with friends.

The microwave beeped,
I threw open the door,
hugged the hot ceramic
in small paws,
raised it to my lips
sipping greedily,
immediately discovering
this revelation
to taste
like mop water
filtered through a dirty gym sock.

I spit it into the sink,
dumped the rest,
flabbergasted at the difference
between smell and taste,
even guzzling a Pepsi
to rid my mouth of the bitterness.

I thought,
*I will never take another sip...*

*Adults must be crazy*
*drinking this stuff...*

Twenty-nine years later,
it's a three-cup habit
and fine pleasure.

# Among the Wastes of Time

By Bill Cushing

<u>1978</u>

Stumbling through hallways muttering,
she pokes a cane in corners, asking,
        "What's that?
        Who's there?"
to empty air.
She's become an inconsistent mind
in an incontinent body. Later,

lying on a bed shielding
hidden cans and dry goods
she herself has forgotten are there,
she whimpers, calling
the name
of her older brother, a man
who in thirty years
has heard nothing.

<u>1986</u>

In an old building an old man, a retired major,
shits in his pants and curses
the insubordinate body that refuses,
anymore, to obey and does as it pleases
when it pleases
in a manner which would shame God Himself.

Later, visiting his wife, two decades dead,
he shakes and frets
on the bench,
surrounded by the tombstones that
protrude from the ground
like fingertips of the buried
fighting to claw their way free of the earth.

# Salt, Thorns, Otis Redding, Why ...

By A. Whittenberg

Salt without bread

Thorns on a cactus

Otis Redding, I miss you

Why didn't you go Greyhound.

# Chincoteague House

By B.A. Brittingham

# Shabbath

By Tali Cohen Shabtai

When I don't have cigarettes,
it determines my
Sabbath fate.

Nevertheless,
it all begins with a cigarette on
Sabbath
with an exhale just
before sunset
until the inhalation
the next day when the stars
emerge
with the blessing "That distinguishes between sacred and
profane"

This is the most important day
to consume cigarettes, because the day when
God rested
from all his work is not an idea.

That every business is closed
in Jerusalem, even if they made
enough from tobacco
consumption during the week.

Really, there's a woman for whom the cigarette is
her language
and the way she counts
in cigarette butts
corrects her phobia
with numbers.

I need a cigarette that does not exceed 10 centimeters and is
no more than 7 millimeters in diameter
The effect of the nicotine substance found in tobacco on the
human brain
inspires in me at the same time
the quality of writing on the Sabbath.

It should be seriously considered


that there are withdrawal
symptoms arising from a lack of
nicotine in the brain that is prevented from me
to contain them
when a person does not consume cigarettes
on the Holy Sabbath.

Accordingly, the biblical saying will come here that
"the Sabbath may be broken when life is at stake"

Should I silence any thirst
and adhere with the Creator blessed without
any adherence to an object
for an entire day?

Generally the week enters on the Sabbath.
For me? On Sunday.

# Untiled

By Derek Roper

# Traveller M. In the Land of the Cynocephali

By Bob Mimpriss

> the 'colonised do not know how to breathe'…
> 'the people here don't know how to walk; they
> make tiny little steps which don't get them
> ahead.'
>
> Albert Memmi, *The Coloniser and the Colonised*

A child slips down from its mother's lap, and toddles between
the empty tables to where I am sitting. I feel myself stiffen at
her approach, looking down at the grey-check tablecloth and
my tea until she clambers onto the seat opposite mine at the
bark of her mother's waning. I glance up. She is wearing a
tee-shirt showing the characters from some Hollywood
children's film, with a dolly-bead necklace round her neck,
and as my eyes meet hers, the jaw drops open, showing
pointed teeth, and the long tongue flicks at the end of the
nose. I keep very still, hardly daring to breathe. Again there is
a bark from her mother, and a waitress passing in front of my
table stops and offers her hand to the child with a grunt of
invitation. She glances over her shoulder at me as she does so,
her long-fingered left hand with its wedding ring scratching at
the point where her fur lightens over the muzzle, and leads
the child away down the aisle towards her mother. For a
moment we have been the centre of attention. A robed man a
few tables down yaps a few remarks to his wife, and laps
from his drinking bowl. The atmosphere in the breakfast
room returns to normal: the growl of Cynocephalic voices,
the smell of tobacco and of cooking fat from the heater, the
steam cooling on the windows, the cold.

The girl's mother is one of a crowd which gathers
round the heater every morning. Neither staff nor guests,

they come into the breakfast room off the street in their outdoor clothes, and sit and drink tea from their thermos flasks or illicit vodka from unmarked bottles while they warm themselves: the indigent, the lazy and the unemployed claiming the traditional rights of nomads on the steppe. More reserved, since they prefer to sit apart from each other and at tables towards the door, are the professionals in robes or western suits, up from the smaller cities on business, and a little suspicious of the engineers and geologists with whom they share this hotel. At present there are just three of us. The Russian bends over his dumplings and gravy at a table closer to the heater than mine; the Dutchman is eating salted mutton behind me, at a table by the door. The hotel is shunned by foreign workers because of its Cynocephalic menu: meat and vegetables and vodka are served in abundance, but amidst the bitter, the salt and the sour, the human tongue yearns for sweetness. Perhaps, like me, the Russian and Dutchman long to move to the Marriott or the Hilton closer to the centre; perhaps they feel abandoned here by their employers as some obscure penalty for some unknown offence. If so, they are wise to avoid me, for there is guilt in association. I have been here for longer than any other guest; I have been in this hotel for almost six weeks.

An accordion partition separates the breakfast room from the foyer, where the receptionist sits and reads his paper in the slack half hour before checkout, and where the sliding doors roll endlessly open and closed, a problem which will be repaired, so I am told, when a replacement control mechanism is available. The lift works, if anything in the land of the Cynocephali works, but the lurching and groaning of its motor is such that I prefer to use the staircase by the foyer. My bedroom overlooks parkland to the rear of the hotel. The carpet and bedding are of unbleached wool, while the walls are painted a light grey that to a race without colour vision is soothing. A few pictures of hunting scenes, hieroglyphic and stylised, adorn the walls, the famous Cynocephalic line art. The radiator looks new, but the room is cold at night, and I spread my coat over the counterpane and watch the late shows with the sound turned low while I drink rice or potato vodka from the convenience store down the road. In the two dimensions of the TV, Cynocephalic life is reduced to a children's cartoon. Suited pundits lounge in black leather chairs and give their verdicts on current affairs, muzzles raised and ears cocked in consideration of each others' whining. Celebrities in fashionable Western dress preside over their talk shows and game shows, heads to one side, tongues lolling at the hilarity. Footballers, surgeons, labourers, policemen — all are made ridiculous by the grinning, panting faces of dogs.

Our conversations are bilingual. I address the Cynocephali in halting Chinese or Russian, and they reply in their own tongue: they can study any language on earth, but they speak no language except their own. In this juxtaposition of the foreign and the alien I learn that my radiator is cold because water pressure in the city is low; that there are warmer rooms downstairs if I wish to ask my employers to upgrade me; that the warmer bedding I asked for has been ordered, and will be delivered soon, and in the meantime, perhaps I can suggest to my employers that they pay a small advance on my bill… Cynocephalic grammar does not lend itself to accountability. We engage, not as receptionist and guest, but as representatives of our kinds; it is impossible to tell whether the cold in my room is the responsibility of the receptionist, or the hotel staff, or the whole of the Cynocephalic nation, while my simple demand for warmer bedding becomes a diplomatic problem of sprawling complexity, a matter of providing bedding for the Androcephalic race.

Yet it is not that they have no history of dealing with the outside world. Egyptian art depicts them, a fragment of Old Welsh poetry deals with them, and Scandinavian legend tells of a Cynocephalus installed by the conquering Swedes as their puppet king of Norway. They were conscripted by Genghis Khan on his expansion into the west, fought as mercenaries in the armies of the Turks, and later joined the Roma people on their wanderings into Europe, leaving small settlements scattered across Central Asia and as far as the Carpathian Alps. Meanwhile, in the Land of the Cynocephali (which like the Basque Country or the Palestinian Territories has no name except that), they have repelled the Russians, the Mongolians, and the Chinese; and now, with the help of foreign investment and expertise, they expand their cities, build airports and roads, and begin to extract the rare earths that will modernise their economy, and make it possible, perhaps, to heat my room and provide an extra blanket for my bed. Meanwhile, outside the hotel, in their filthy and sprawling capital city, in government offices, ticket offices, libraries and shops, I encounter the same badly maintained machinery, the same cold and the smell of cooking oil, the same bureaucratic indifference to it all.

I have heard a rumour that they are selling wine today in one of the shops trading in dollars with the Androcephali, so I will look in there once I have visited the Ministry of Labour to see if my work permit is ready. After shopping, I will call on my employers, where if I have my work permit I can move into an office and start work, and if not, mention that advance on my hotel bill, and ask to be upgraded to a warmer room. When I have finished my errands in town, I will have dinner at the restaurant opposite the hotel, and perhaps watch a film on one of the American channels before I turn out my light. I get on the trolley-bus by the railway bridge round the corner, and I sit behind three teenagers with skateboards, and shiver as it inches its way into town, stopping for labourers on their way between building sites; housewives and school-children with dust masks over their muzzles as though someone fears they might bite; and, like stray dogs, the same ragged kind who congregate in the breakfast room for the mere chance to sit somewhere warm. Meanwhile, the city grinds past my window: a boarding school where children taken from nomads on the steppe are trained to work as waiters and cleaners in the city; old cottages shaped like tumuli still clinging among the tower blocks; the city's first American church, and everywhere, new buildings — their colours drab or stark in appeal to the colourless eyes of the Cynocephali, or streaked and splashed at random with imported paints.

I get off at the edge of the Silk Merchants' Quarter a few minutes' walk from the Ministry.

A man is roasting a marmot over a brazier formed from an oil barrel. As I pass, he bastes it with oil from a jug, and the young man in front of me stops abruptly, his muzzle raised with a rapt look: a cartoon dog sniffing the cartoon air. I step round him, and into the path of three young women, emerging from the new Gucci store with their shopping bags in their hands. Another food stall is selling pigs' trotters and beef tea, and a businessman crosses the street with a paper drinking bowl in his hand, yapping into his mobile phone. I cross the main road into wooded parkland. A light snow is falling, and a white-collared crow struts across my path, and takes flight towards a line of elms. The memorial to some warrior hero has been defaced by a graffiti artist's scrawl, and as I pass the outdoor swimming pool I see the rough sleepers under the galleries. One of them raises his head as I pass, and I see that he is human. And something in his gaze — not appeal, not even self-pity, but the simple acceptance of suffering — weighs down my shoulders as I climb the steps into the Ministry of Labour.

A long, rather dusty hallway with a waiting area at the near end and officials seated behind desks at the far. Beside the entrance, a machine dispensing numbered tickets, and opposite, a mural depicting more industry and progress than I have seen in the land of the Cynocephali since I arrived. Voices, blurred and obscure. From the officials at the far end, the grunts and growls of hopes deferred, requests denied, rising in attacks of bureaucratic annoyance, and drowned out at intervals by the bark of the tannoy calling the next ticket holder forward. On galleries lined with bookshelves, runners weaving past each other with files to be taken downstairs for reference or upstairs to be re-shelved, a system unchanged since the days of gas lighting. And competing with all this, the yapping and mewling of those who have come to find work, or to plead that they cannot work, or that there is no work to find. I take my ticket, and sit down on the nearest bench. A woman edges away from me, drawing the folds of her lurid green dress beneath her, her gaze averted: does she find my flat and hairless ape's face as discomforting as I find hers? Then a bark from the tannoy that makes me jump, and a double amputee wheels past me in his chair, a relic of Communist days, and no doubt of Communist wars. I could sit here for an hour, three hours, and again I could leave empty-handed: the simple stamped permit that is all I require seems as far beyond the capacities of this place as the digitisation of its records. The Cynocephali think nothing of waiting. A whole family sit on the floor by the oil burner, eating dumplings and blood sausage sliced with a knife; two old men near them are playing billiards on the floor. And then, as the amputee wheels his way back towards the exit, someone breaks into song. It is a low drone at first, incessant and desolate, joined by other notes that break and merge in microtonal harmonies, the famous polyphonic overtones of Cynocephalic keening. The singer seems not even to breathe. Yet after a few moments he falls silent, and another singer elsewhere in the hall takes up the song with not even a pause, with not even a hint that this dirge need ever end. It catches my breath. And for an hour I sit there, scarcely moving as singer after singer takes the note, listening to themes that my mind can barely follow though they haunt me, as aloof and moving as the howling of wolves.

I have been to the shop that sells Androcephalic produce, where I bought three bottles of Uzbek wine, and I have been to my employers to ask if they can help obtain my work permit or are willing to pay an advance on my bill. I sat in the senior manager's office in a leather mahogany chair, as I explained that the Ministry of Labour have not stamped my work permit because the Ministry of the Interior have not released my entry papers, while the aged Cynocephalus under whose direction I will work poured salted tea into two lacquered drinking bowls. There was a pause. He pushed my bowl across the table towards me, apologising for the lack of sugar and milk. Perhaps, he said, the Ministry of Labour will have my work permit ready tomorrow, or perhaps I can call at the Ministry of the Interior to see if my entry papers are there; and in the mean time, he assured me, the room at the hotel is mine. I mentioned the cold in my room, and the hotel's request for an advance on my bill. His ears pricked, a show of surprise. The company was paying my bill weekly, he said; could it be that the hotel were mistaken? No doubt there had been some delay at the bank, some mistake in their records, unfortunate but easily rectified. He would ask the accounts department to make due enquiries. His staff would contact theirs. And since my duties would be cared for by his existing staff until my situation was clearer, I could do worse than to spend my time in language study, or take one of the coach tours into the hinterland so I can see what the Cynocephalic people are achieving for their beautiful country. A recitation of one of the epics begins at the Opera House tonight: the country's most famous epic vocalist, accompanied by the state chorale — perhaps he will see me there?

He rose, and shook my hand with infinite courtesy.

I was assaulted on the way home. Three youths, leaning with their backs to the wall under the railway bridge, waited until I was passing them and tripped me up, kicked me in the hip as I lay on the cobblestones and clutched my bag, and scattered with barks of delight. I was not robbed. The attack had no purpose I can understand. Yet if I were to report the matter to the local police, if I were to give a description of my assailants (the upper lip curled back to reveal the fangs of the one who kicked me, the cocked left ear of the one who tripped me first), I would convey nothing more, perhaps, than my own confusion, and my own rising hate and fear of this country... The hoodie was *red,* sir; what

125

texture is that? And were the kids who assaulted you black or white?

I lie in bed with the TV on, rubbing the bruise on my hip, when I am overwhelmed by longing for human faces and human speech. The channel is religious, its presenters slick with the power of dollars and God, and I raise my glass to the screen in wry salute. And then it strikes me. If a cat wandered onto the set, would these dog-heads cast the new religion aside? Would they leap from their chairs on all fours, tongues lolling, would they drive it from the studio in the ecstasy of the chase? Catch her, Mr Peanut Butter! Get her, Trixie Woo! The snow is thick outside now, and I am giggling at my tasteless joke as I gulp down the Uzbek wine.

# NorthCalif #3

By B.A. Brittingham

# Kids In Port Patrick Harbour
By Dave Medd

Jumping off the end of a granite pier -
the show-off, me-first, me-as-well;
the nonchalant what's-it-all-about, and the one
who won't be shown up by his mates. One
with poems instead of courage who waits
too long but goes for it anyway. Last of all
the small one, tiny brother, limbs like
tent-pole insects, whippersnapper, chipping at
the edges of rhyme, who's gonna do it just one time while
dad is watching.

And the girls.

Long, thin girls in wet, black suits.
Every bit as good as the boys
this one, and two with hair still way past their waists,
longing to take the plunge not knowing
would this be back to a world of street games,
smudged calculations in exercise books,
chewed nails and split ends? Or
into deep water murk, so green,
nothing to see till you're in there over your head,
crabs and lobsters, concealed rocks and hazards,
maybe a pirate or two with his treasure
and bones?

So two hold hands and leap out squealing
out into air, into fast, clean air.
And velvet scoters, not really found in our region,
race like smutty black ambulances
to the very spot where they disappeared.

# Babysitting Our Niece

By Robert Cooperman

When our niece was two or three,
her parents needed some time alone,
so they asked Beth and me to babysit.
They weren't gone five minutes
when she woke, and beholding us, wailed,

"I want my mama!" convinced
she'd been abandoned, no matter how we tried
to reassure her, to trick her with toys, treats,
the TV she could stare at for hours,
as if tiny gods were trapped inside.

We tried rocking her, singing to her,
cooing to her as if to a love bird.
I recited every poem I'd memorized.
Nothing. Just her sobbing,
Beth and I close to tears, as well,
praying for blessed quiet: in my case,
at least, retribution for those Saturday nights

my parents wanted, with the desperation
of their exhausted week, to enjoy
a restaurant dinner, a movie, or dancing,
while I howled, knowing they'd never
come back once they'd escaped the tiny despot
they'd allowed to rule, to ruin, their lives.

# Window Pane

By Beatrice Georgalidis

## "Window Pane"

By Mark Blickley

It was time for Ralph's first real haircut. Ralph's mother said it was time, as did the next-door parents of his best friend, Emmitt. The only person who did not think it was time for a real haircut was Ralph. He did not want to go to the barbershop.

Ralph liked having his mother cut his hair. Last month she was so tired after working a double shift at the hospital she accidently sliced his ear with the scissors. There was a lot of blood. On Sunday Mother announced that Bright's Barber Shop had finally opened after being closed for nearly four months because of the virus. She scheduled an appointment for Ralph on Friday.

Thursday night Ralph could not fall asleep. Every time he shut his eyes all he could see was the huge window in front of Mr. Bright's barbershop. Ralph hated that window. He had to pass it every week when his mother took him to the babysitter before she went to work at St. Ann's Medical Center.

Even though Ralph hated the window, he would always look inside as he passed by. He couldn't help himself. And what he saw truly frightened him. A large bald-headed man with a bushy moustache named Mr. Bright was always chopping off somebody's hair. Ralph remembered seeing men, boys, and even a lady tied to a chair, looking like prisoners as Mr. Bright danced around them waving sharp tools.

Friday morning Ralph was very very nervous and refused to leave the house. He felt as trapped as the frogs he stalked, caught and tossed into his pail. For the first time in his life Ralph wished he were a frog. Frogs don't have hair.

# Ser 2

By Carmen Caro

# Sing Child

By K.P. Heyming

Sing child
of new and soul of old.
Your voice is not yet
hoarse or bitter. It is
loud, and clear, and
unapologetic about
the things it carries
with it.
Sing child
of sweet melodies
and warm memories,
and of the truths so many
have tried to silence
in you.
Sing child
of caged lips and shackled
teeth that keep
everyone' secrets beneath
though you are the only one
suffering the sentence.
Sing child
of the love, and the hurt, and
the hate, and the hope
of stories that cannot
be told without whimsy
for fear of failing
the fairy tale.
Sing child
and be quiet no more.

# Blue Streak

By Dave Medd

*Coo-ee!*

*You and me, Sputnik,*
*Atlas, Vostok,*
*heave a brick, beatnik,*
*Jupiter, Voskhod,*
*take your pick, oh my God!*

*Titan, Soyuz,*
*rock and mod, down the nick,*
*it's down to us, give it stick,*
*give it welly, spare the rod,*
*it must be,*
*cos we've seen it on the telly.*

It was a time of rockets; we all flew together;
wasteland flares of innocence, bound for the blue obscure;
each dawn they trailed their day-glow sparkles, tracing lifelines
over the wrinkly hand of God.

This was our script; we could pretend; our catch-me-please games
ran wide over world and land we were making our own;
old gods, on rickety thrones in an innocent blue,
grumbled on lost ground; exotic

parables danced from the east, on shivering trembles.
New morning promised a terrible, table-thumping
uncle mischief, a mystical union, murmur-sweet

comforting for us.

Everywhere, nose-cone caricature, cylindrical
futures dangled their lures, zipped on invisible wires
and fuses, confounding rock-beat, heartbeat musical,
fairytale acid blossom.

We tiptoed round our war of worlds, new jazz, lollipops,
harried a crater's mass of grey possibilities;
each weekend, wash-house bath by the fire; like seaside trips
we journeyed into wild space.

Soon, whenever we fell, there was always the doctor;
in a time of rockets, the only way is up.

# Three Acts

By Allison Whittenberg

My children drowned. 16 months ago. 2 years ago. 6 years ago.

My children, just as naked, as now, just as submerged back when we moved through the uncertainty of shelters, sustaining by government crumbs, their father is not my husband.

The voices talk, pharmaceutical extractions mute the voice shout.

Are there sharks under the golden gate?

I drive to the bridge God is there, but he blinks I strip my babies and listen to the smell of the bay. It fills me, the soft rays illuminate. I do it again. Once more.

In your news reports, please include: I'm drowning too.

# Nancy Tolliver Buys Girl Scout Cookies Outside the Wild Weed Dispensary: Denver

By Robert Cooperman

> "The Girl Scouts of Colorado have decided it's now
> cool to peddle their baked goods outside marijuana
> dispensaries."—*The Denver Post*

My Harold loves these cookies with almost
the adoration we'd have lavished
on children, had we been so blessed.
He has so few pleasures, my poor love, I left him
with the hospice nurse—who whispered it might
be better if I bought some marijuana for him,
for pain management—and drove here fast,
and buy three of every flavor, but I fear he'll just stare,
with the longing Keats must've felt in his last, sad days.

How we loved to quote his poems on our Scottish
walking tour in his footsteps, but ventured farther north,
and not sleeping rough; clean sheets and a luxurious bath
at the end of each day's hikes, Harold massaging
my soles with his all-knowing fingers.

Keats had his companion Severn place books around
his last bed in Rome, so if he couldn't read them,
could at least feel their beauty and wisdom seep
from their pages into his brain, heart, and soul.

Maybe that's what Harold wants, now that everything
tastes of ashes, of dust and dirt, though I pray
these cookies will magic a cure for my darling.

## Thomas Bickerstaff Buys Girl Scout Cookies Outside the Wild Weed Dispensary: Denver

By Robert Cooperman

"The Girl Scouts of Colorado have decided it's now
cool to peddle their baked goods outside marijuana
dispensaries."—*The Denver Post*

It's about time,
but they're thinking too small,
like, well, like little girls,
and not a man with big ideas.

If it were me, and it will be,
they'd be selling all kinds
of munchies, not just cookies,
but brownies, marinara sauce,
and all of it laced with pot,
plus T-shirts, posters
of pop stars in Scout uniforms,
a button or two undone,
to show some creamy ta-ta's
to appeal to stoners,
who get so crazy on a few tokes
they need instant gratification.

I almost feel like tossing away
the lid I just bought—or wait,
selling it to one of these parents
too tightly wrapped to sneak
into the Wild Weed
while their kids flog cookies—

to concentrate, instead,
on creating a company name,
logo, a marketing strategy,
and to find suppliers, designers,
seamstresses, to make tchotchkes
to my specifications.

Free enterprise!  Capitalism!
Selling everything to everybody!
What makes this country great!

# The Walk
By Mike Nichols

That September our plow horse lay down and her gut twisted and she died. So when Caroline, my little angel, took sick there was nothing for it but to walk to Pashto for medicine. Though it was near November there was hardly any snow yet, but Molly knew that there soon would be, and so she agonized over my leaving. Caroline was getting no better after three days, during which Molly had fought against the child's killing fever. We could do no more for her and there was no doctor near. Not by a jug full could I stand idly by and watch her be taken from us.

We'd come west from Baltimore to Missouri Territory with our mare, Betsy, a few chickens, a goat for the milk she gave, and our wagon loaded with our few possessions. After six years married Molly and me thought we could never have children. So, after less than a year spent here in the territory, Caroline's coming was quite a surprise and a double joy to us.

Molly fixed me up with bacon, salt pork, boiled eggs, and corn cakes for the walk. I dressed as warmly as I could in my shell jacket and frayed woolen sack coat. I kissed them both good-bye, but my Caroline was delirious with fever and she said, "Papa? It is too hot in here. I want to go outside now to sit and splash in the creek."

I did not believe she really knew I was there and it made me teary to see her in such a state. So I tramped off for Pashto with a sad yet hopeful heart.

I stepped out on the plank walk and the heavy door to the apothecary slammed behind me. The sound of it echoed long and loud in the cold air. I patted the pocket of my sack coat again for the feel of the flat brown bottle of medicine. The memory of the three days spent in the widow Spencer's corn crib watching the snow fall and waiting for the medicine to arrive were a torment to me. The fear of what those wasted days might mean for my Caroline chattered at my mind.

I had never imagined that I might have to wait for a new shipment of medicine to arrive in Pashto. There had been a lot of sickness already that year. The apothecary said that the contents of the brown bottle would help stop my little Caroline's coughing fits. He'd also given me packets of powders for her fever and the swelling in her throat which made it hard for her to breath.

I tried to beg the loan of a horse but I was not known in Pashto, and so I was treated as a malingerer and often told to go boil my shirt. I thought to take a horse under cover of night. I would bring it back after Caroline was well again. But, if I were caught, I would have been strung up from the nearest oak and been of no good to her. There was nothing else for it. I would tramp back home as fast as I was able. I looked to the west and the dark clouds bunched there. It would snow again, maybe. I screwed down my slouch hat and pulled up the rough collar of my coat against the chill air and stepped off the plank walk.

I left Pashto behind and was soon tramping through snow which was in some places drifted high as my knees. I walked and the morning wore away. When my left foot pushed uneven through the snow my knee buckled hard. I ignored the pain and forged on. The cold air stung my eyes and seeped through that sack coat. I counseled myself that to keep moving was the key, slow and steady, not so fast that the sweat would break out on my skin. I kept moving and recalled Caroline's lively conversation by the fire.

I stumbled a bit coming down an uneven slope and a black dog stepped from a stand of poplar to the North. I was startled by how it stood out against the snow, an aberration. It was an average-sized mongrel with a head too large for its body. It stared at me through black eyes and I stopped and stared back. When I began walking again, the black dog stepped out from the dark trees and walked out to me. It fell in behind me and matched my pace. I thought that it must live on a homestead nearby and that it would turn and head back soon. I tried to ignore it. I looked back every so often, always expecting it would be gone, but always it was there two paces behind me. Its front feet and legs were thick, it was black as midnight, and there was no other spot of color on it.

I stopped and I turned to shoo the dog off several times, but it only sat in the snow and cocked its head to stare at me as if I were some form of wonderment. It showed no sign that it meant to leave me. So in the end I told it, "Have it your way, but I got a long slog ahead, and you'll likely regret it."

As the afternoon wore on I kept looking back, now almost afraid that the dog would not be there. It would look up to meet my eyes each time I turned, then it would lower its head to stare at my feet. I was glad not to be alone with only thoughts of my little Caroline and of those three days wasted and gone. The brown bottle of amber liquid sloshed in my pocket. I unbuttoned my coat and reached in to touch it, to know that it was safe.

I was getting tired but dared not admit it. Fear crept in and told me that I would not make it back through snow this deep. I pushed such thoughts from my head and concentrated on my footsteps instead. I remembered the loaf of bread and the ham wrapped in cheese cloth in my coat. I tore off pieces of each and chewed them in the cold as I walked. I drank the water from my gourd, the chill of it an unwelcome reminder of the dropping temperature.

The sun was low behind the clouds, and I half-expected the dog to stop or to turn back, but it did not. Always it stayed two paces behind me in the trail I broke in the snow. Its step and breath and body comforted me.

I had taken three days and two nights with brief rest to make my way to Pashto, but there had been much less snow then. Thoughts of the three days waiting in the corncrib crept into my mind again, and a sick feeling wrapped around my guts. I groaned and stumbled and fell to my hands and knees in the snow. I knew that my worrying did no good, yet I was powerless to stop. Worry had wrapped its way all through me. I looked back and the dog sat in the snow watching me. It looked away as if embarrassed to be caught staring. Its pink tongue fell loose over its big jaw and it panted and looked off into the distance.

The sun would soon be gone. An image of Caroline sweating and moaning beneath the patchwork quilt while Molly dabbed at her head with a wet cloth sprang to my mind, and I scrambled to my feet. I felt like a schoolboy caught at doing something bad. I got to feeling crazy, and I started to run to make up for lost time. I came to my senses and chastised myself out loud. I knew I must not tire myself out like that.

I unbuttoned my coat and for a moment my numb fingers could not feel the bottle. I fought down the panic and stuck my hands in the coat under my arms and when they'd warmed a little I could feel the bottle. I cursed myself for a fool.

The sun was gone and with it the clouds. The cold was stinging and brutal. My legs ached but my feet were numb. To regain feeling in them I would stop and stomp them every little while. I recalled times when Caroline would walk beside me as I plowed. She'd talk to me of everything and of nothing. I did not look back to see if the dog was there, but I felt its presence. I began to feel as if it were driving me.

At Broke-Leg Creek I spent a long while chipping a hole in the ice. I filled the gourd and drank. The dog drank, and I filled the gourd again. I fell into a stupor, staring off at nothing until the dog's whining broke the spell. I pushed up off my knees and patted that brown bottle in my pocket, solid and reassuring, and I started off again.

The moon rose and made its low arch across the dark frozen sky. It would fall below the horizon soon. I wanted to rest, and I damned myself for my weakness. I saw my little Caroline, pale white, brittle dry and shivering in her pallet beneath the patchwork quilt. I cried out and the dog whined and I stumbled and fell. I sobbed then, once. I cursed myself out loud for behaving like a little milksop. I pushed myself up and made my aching legs move.

The dawn came colder than the night. The sun was blinding, but it gave no warmth. I walked. The dog's presence always behind me, a persistent persuasive force. My legs grew so tired lifting up out of the snow and crunching back down into it. Footfalls without end. Mostly I looked down at the snow just in front of me, only glancing up from time to time, realigning myself westerly.

Hunger dug at my belly, and I ate as I walked while the moon slowly dropped in its arch to the South. I pulled more of the ham and the last of the dry bread from my coat and chewed it slowly. I looked back at the dog and it looked up at me. I tossed it a hard heel of bread, then a hunk of ham, and it bolted them both down.

The clouds returned and with them some warmth but also a fear of snow and what that would mean. The food brought me no strength, and I would drift into a half sleep while I walked. I would wake with a start only to drift off again while my legs moved beneath me, loose, weary and disjointed.

The sun was low behind the clouds again when the dog drove me to Moose-Rib creek. The water was swift so that I did not have to break ice. I unstoppered and filled my gourd, and the dog and I drank. I filled the gourd again and it was time to move but my legs wouldn't lift me. I felt that I was done.

Then the dog bit me. I lay on my side in the soft snow, sleeping. It bit my hand hard but I could not rouse myself. It barked and whined in my ear. It butted me hard in the face with its wet nose, and the vision of a tiny grave sparked in my mind, of a pure white cairn of rocks and of snow falling and of cold. I rolled and rose and took two steps but fell again. The dog barked and leapt at me. I told it, "I know it." I got my feet under me again, and after some time my legs found a shambling rhythm.

The cold came when the sun went. I shivered endlessly. I slapped my arms and chest and stamped my feet until I was too tired to do it any longer. The dog seemed to know when my energy flagged for at those moments it barked, sharp and piercing, and nudged the back of my leg with its blunt nose. I cursed myself for a weakling, and I prayed to God for strength though I thought it unlikely that He cared aught for the troubles of a pitiful creature such as me. I thought of my small darling girl and asked only for strength to get back to her.

I tore the last of the ham in two and handed the dog its share and thus our second night of walking passed with me stumbling, sleeping, and falling, and the dog biting, barking and nudging.

Another frozen dawn came. My exposed face stung but my feet felt warm, and I knew I might lose some toes. I did not care how far I had yet to go, only that I must keep going. I saw Boney Mountain off in the west and knew that I had strayed off course and that with another day's walking, I still would not be home. I grasped the brown bottle through my coat and I looked back at the dog. It stared at me, by its existence it goaded me on.

We walked away the morning and my mind would not work right. Thoughts drifted up and out without meaning. I suffered through dreams and mirages of warmth. Roaring fires spat glowing embers inside tight chinked cabins. Buckets of steaming scalding water poured in a tin wash tub. Sunny green hillocks roiled with heat waves.

I awoke in annoyance with my face pressed into the snow and Caroline's laughter in my ears. The black dog chewed and pulled on my leg. It tore through my pants and bruised my flesh, but I could not rouse myself to stop it. It gripped a finger through my glove and bit until the cartilage popped, and I cried out and rolled onto my back.

The dog sat in the snow watching me. It washed my face with its warm tongue and I remembered. Tears welled in my eyes. I spoke, "You must stand and move though you are a pitiable weakling." Then I stood.

The pain in my hips and knees was a horror, and the dog barked shrilly and leapt and twisted in front of me. I took a step and thought that I would fall. The dog jumped at my face and nipped me under the eye, like a blow from a fist. I rushed to give it a kick but instead I fell into a stumbling drunken pace, and the dog took its place behind me. It would, from time to time, run in front of me twisting to glare at me and bark. It was an awful piercing noise. It carried the same effect as a slap for me.

The sun was gone. The cold was a misery. I held tight to the bottle through my coat as we walked, and I thought of my little Caroline, soon to be hale and hardy with this good medicine inside her. Surely we could walk a few more hours now after all we'd done already. A few more hours and I would hold my little angel tight and kiss her lovely face.

I'd fallen again, and the dog was barking. I got to my knees, and I wavered. I saw the ridge on my right where Dan Collin's burnt out place had been. I could make it home now. I was that close. The night was warming. I could smell the snow in the air and then it came, huge wet flakes, but I was on the last leg now, coming up Copper Ridge. Sometimes I stumbled and fell, and sometimes I crawled. Then I would curse myself, and the dog would lick my face as if to strip away skin, and I'd stand and stumble on.

I could see the dark shape of the home place ahead. Oh, my joy! I cackled like a madman and said to the dog, "We have made it!"

I fell through the door and staggered to Caroline's empty pallet. Well, I thought, she must be fine now, I'd worried for nothing. Ha! The joke was on me. She hadn't needed any apothecary's potions to get her through. She'd beat it all on her own.

Well then, I'd thought, she must be hiding, the little imp. I turned, and I saw Molly's stunned and stricken face and knew I had it wrong. My Caroline, my only one, was washed and dressed and wrapped in clean linen in the cooling shed where she'd lain those last three nights. Where she'd wait 'til spring when the ground would thaw enough to open for her small grave, her cairn of white stones.

I stumbled outside into the white world of falling snow to look for the black dog, but it was gone. I had no name for it so I could only cry out, "Black dog!" over and again until I dropped to my knees, exhausted, and wept. I wept for my little angel now gone to heaven, for the dog lost in the falling snow.

I never found the dog. I wanted to repay it somehow. Since then I've sometimes wondered, as I go about my work in the warm spring air and recall the bygone melody of Caroline's sweet voice in her rambling conversations, if the dog had been at all.

# A Look Into Us

By Steven Rossi

I write letters in tongue
about the man who mirrors my unknowing
and gambles on the odds of seeing myself.

I was born of ontology the day he asked me
"Do you like the way you look?"
while aiming our mirror to the light of another day.

I father faith in precepts
in the images looking back at me,
each possible and true in its own light.

With logs in my eyes I call him religion
and worship from a temple of shards,
etching my misspellings of perfection
with the sharpest edges
into its better shadows,

just as God kept nightfall
the day He created light.

Until then I write each letter as a prayer
then cast them over the shadows
where our mirror lost us
until 'perfection' begins to look like 'tomorrow'

# Come Within

By Perla Kantarjian

in the house of language
many forms are birthed through.

simple: look
at something, anything,
and say no earthly word.

press the words into your guts,
churn them powerful into senses.

there are too many spoken things
here, yet not enough thoughts given to language tugging the truth
of emotion forward.

for instance: immerse expansive in the perfect
of the eyes. the absorption of sights
tender on the spirit. and be left full. satiated. Stricken
with your own senses.

in the redness of your stream flows a verbal intricacy
of its full own. formulating in liquid.
ceaselessly.

listen well to the sentences
you construct to address your very self.

beware they don't end up
burdening your blood, clotting.

# A Routine Group
By David Subacchi


Before a mirror my actions

Do not match,

I raise this hand

The silent glass

Raises the other,

I frown in frustration

A face smiles,

I have to struggle

To recognise it,

My skin is dark

White looks back,

I breathe

The image chokes,

I turn away,

Silently

Behind me

Someone stands

Laughing loudly.


In crowds I attract

Little attention,

A thousand eyes

Categorise me

As one who belongs

To a routine group,

Commonplace,

Not dangerous

In stable

Circumstances,

Am I recognised

For what I am

Or what others

Imagine me to be,

There is no way

To be certain,

Shop windows

Stare mockingly.

# I will Call You In The Morning

By Thomas Zampino

I carried you up the stairs trying not to wake you. But the steps were rebellious and had other ideas. With every movement forward they released a rheumatic sigh.

Your curly brown hair gently rubbed across my arms while your breath stayed in close rhythm with my own. Slow, and steady, and light.

I placed you down on your bed, the one you would soon outgrow.

A quick kiss before I left. More of a promise, really, than some remnant of the night. I needed you to know that I would be here when you wake.

Even now, I account for every one of those tomorrows.

Your room may be empty but my promises never were.

I will call you in the morning.

# Did it prevent your sun-kissed dreams?

By Mark Andrew Heathcote


Father that sundial, is it death
is it Father - the hand of death?
Is it the sword that cuts short a bird's flight?

'Child, we're all adjacent, the window of life.'

'It's a window of infinite-endless light.'

O' Father is it a guillotine
do it covert our breath.
O' Father how much time,
time-does-we have left?

'Child, we're all adjacent, the window of life
until the bird in your soul takes flight.'

'Child, a question …answer your father this.
Did it prevent your sun-kissed dreams? Last night.'

# Korean Retro Day

By CJP Lee

# Into Muted Dusk

By Lorraine Caputo

By day's end
the sky is a washed-
indigo blue above
the desert cliffs

Seafog has settled
revealing faint silhouettes
of further mountains

The waves have grown
larger, their tide
high, their crush
louder

On the *malecón* & on
the dunes gather couples
one in a tangled embrace

The sun sets, a
brilliant mango swallowed
by the platinum-
blue sea

A pastel spectrum paints the
horizon & quickly fades
into muted dusk

# It Is Nightfall

By Mark Andrew Heathcote

It is nightfall
hymns to the silence soothe me.
Rain tinkles on terracotta tiles
an owl hoot by the railway line;
a milk float approaches quietly,
and a poem self-seeds itself;
adjusting like a flower to absorb more heat.
And yet I cannot sleep-
for fear, I might bend like a head of wheat
overripe - too heavy,
weighed down by own, unending conceit.
It is nightfall
and even a poet must one day sleep
meet his midnight
and let better hymns to the silence speak
and embroil on the lips

of those best left to mildew weep

# Bike Lock

By John Tavares

When Jordan awoke in the morning, he decided that for the first time in his life in Toronto, which was not his hometown, he would drive across the city, as opposed to commuting on public transit, since he had obtained his driver's license at Adam's insistence and had the use of his partner's second, favorite car. He discovered on the driveway beside the neatly manicured front lawn a young woman, dressed entirely in black denim, tight dark trousers with rolled cuffs, a shortcut jacket, shackled by the neck with a bike lock, cuffed to Adam's car. Somehow, she fastened the bicycle lock to her thin neck, wrapped the bar around handle of Adam's Tesla electric car, and locked the U-bolt there.

The whole move to Adam's place in Toronto and the abandonment of his hometown in Northern Ontario was beginning to seem like a surreal dream. He was staying alone in a house belonging to a man soon to be his husband, and it boggled his mind that, by virtue of domestic family law, eventually the house would be his—or at least half. Now, with Adam away, he had the stone and brick house to himself—and not just any place but a house in Forest Hills, as opposed to a rented room in the basement of a house belonging to a hard-working immigrant family, which was his traditional and usual humble abode when he lived in the city in the past, including as a college student and artist. As he headed out the door, en route to coffee downtown, before he drove the luxurious Tesla to college to pick up the textbooks for his X-Ray technology program, he had flirted with the idea of dropping out of diagnostic imaging, even though he had yet to attend a single class, in favor of enrolling in the interior decorating program at Humber College. Would he change his mind at the last minute?

Then he discovered a young woman, her head shaved, dressed entirely in black leather and black denim, she was shackled to the door handle of the Tesla, somehow ensnared by the neck. She looked like a hipster, but then so many people he saw these days looked like a hipsters, or even hipsters, since he started hanging out with waspish, conservative types like Adam and his ilk and kin.

When he asked her if everything was all right, she said, "I want to speak to my father."

"That's Adam's car. Adam doesn't have any kids."

"I'm not talking to you."

"Girlfriend, you're shackled by the neck to my partner's car, which I was supposed to drive to school, and you don't want to speak with me? Do you want to talk to the police?"

"No. I want to talk with my father."

"What does you father do for a living, by the way?"

"He's a doctor."

"The neighbour next door, and his neighbour, I was told, are also doctors, so I think you have the wrong house and car."

"I don't think so."

"Do you need a doctor?" Jordan queried.

"I don't think so."

"Do you want me to check with the neighbour—just to be certain?"

"I don't think so," she continued to reply in her robotic monotone.

She was a well-built and pretty girl, he thought, it was difficult not to notice—but, after years of uncertainty and self-doubt, he accepted the fact he was gay, although he felt ambiguous at times. He had no interest in her personally, but wanted to ask her about boyfriends to lighten the mood, but somehow it just didn't seem appropriate.

"Are you sure you don't need a doctor?" Jordan asked.

She sat with her narrow back resting against the driver's door with a bicycle lock shackled to her neck, which certainly must have made for quite a spectacle for anyone driving past. Fortunately, their Forest Hill neighbourhood was quiet, residential, not a major thoroughfare or traffic artery.

"No."

"That can't be very comfortable."

"It isn't."

Jordan thought he should call the police, to be safe, but he was worried about outstanding charges from his slightly radical colleges days, his years at the Ontario College of Art, the memory of which even electroshock could not erase.

Jordan first met Adam when he escaped from the psychiatric ward, where he was detained involuntarily for clinical depression, after he attempted to take his own life. Having escaped downstairs in Mount Sinai for an Irish Cream coffee from the Second Cup, he went to the cafeteria to finish the coffee and read a pocketbook *Helplessness*. Adam showed him the sketch he just bought, a landscape by a member of the Group of Seven, who were Jordan's favorite artists as an adolescent growing up in Northwestern Ontario. Jordan even somehow managed to spill coffee on the sketch, despite the fact he handled the minor masterpiece gingerly. He couldn't believe he would bring the art piece to the hospital, but he wanted to exhibit his new acquisition to his co-workers and staff.

Some of his experimental art, installations, including a fake bomb, created controversy and attracted the attention of law enforcement officials, who pressed charges. He was particularly worried about some mischief charges after the bogus bomb installation, which forced a lung disease fundraiser to cancel a black-tie fundraiser at the modern art museum. Jordan believed the Crown dismissed or dropped the charges, but he wasn't certain or confident.

"I'm going to call Adam."

"You do whatever the heck you have to do."

Not only was she seemingly the saddest persons he ever met—and he met many seriously morose artists in his career as a student and artist—but she was also potty-mouthed, he thought, using the f-bomb several times in a single sentence.

"Are sure you don't want a glass of orange juice or a cup of coffee?"

"No."

"Maybe a raisin bran muffin to munch."

"No."

"Girlfriend, I used to survive on coffee and raisin bran muffins from McDonalds when I was an OCA art student. It's called the senior's breakfast special and it was my primary source of nutrition after I spent most of my summer earnings as a group home worker and a lawn mower operator on tuition textbooks, and art supplies."

Jordan was too chatty for her disposition. She didn't seem interested in either food to eat or stories from his glory days as a ruffian avant-garde artist. Then he wondered, looking again at how she was restrained by the bicycle lock, whether she was even capable of consuming food or drink in this awkward recumbent position.

"I'm going to call Adam."

"You do that."

He took the smartphone, which Adam insisted he have, and tried to take a snapshot of the young woman in black with a shaved head shackled to the door handle of his luxury car. But he wasn't confident he knew how to operate the camera on the smartphone and wondered if he even captured a digital image. He realized again he didn't know how to send a text, never mind attach a photo to a text, although he figured from his experience with desktop computers and laptop computers the procedure shouldn't be difficult. He made a long-distance call on the unlimited calling plan that Adam had bought him, which again he didn't want simply because he didn't like talking on the telephone, never mind the cellphone or a smartphone. He called Adam at the clinic in teaching hospital where he worked downtown on University Avenue, where he practiced medicine. Calling

Adam at the clinic or hospital usually annoyed and even angered the doctor to no end, but Jordan felt he had no choice. His call caught Adam after he made the rounds of the hospital wards on University Avenue. In fact, Adam was in the process of clumsy, slipshod cooking, exploding a bowl of soup in the microwave of the staffroom.

"Adam, there's a young woman shackled to your car door."

"What the fuck?"

Jordan slowly explained the conundrum, the captive car, the rather attractive young woman, who cuffed herself to the doorhandle, which reminded him of his own confused, radical days as a struggling, starving artist, whose lack of proper sleep and nutrition made his work and personality even more confusing and hence even more appealing to some culture vultures. He tried to explain the problem clearly to his partner, who hated drama, but found theatricality and histrionics everywhere, and who insisted on accuracy and succinctness. He did admire Adam for his skills in time management.

"Does she have any explosive devices strapped to her?"

"How am I supposed to know?"

"Check."

Adam returned outside, wondering why she would have explosive devices or weapons attached to her. Then again anything seemed possible, but all he observed was an attractive young woman, dressed entirely in black denim, tight dark jean trousers with rolled cuffs, a shortcut denim jacket. She reminded him of a girl he had a crush on in high school - exactly the sort of girl that attracted him, a confused skinny anorexic who couldn't accept he was queer. He updated Adam on the telephone.

"Then call the police."

"Are you certain you want to get the police involved?"

"What else is there to do?"

"Find a bike thief or a mechanic. Don't bike thieves know how to break bike locks, with those cans of freon. I mean, really," Jordan exclaimed. To his annoyance, Jordan found himself making effeminate gestures he swore he'd banish from his repertoire of mannerisms and tics forever.

"Call 911."

"Then the police will become involved, and her life will be ruined if they decide to press charges—something we may not have control over."

To Jordan, she started to appear unreactive and lethargic, increasingly unwell, as her pallor grew ashen. But Jordan could not make a diagnosis – he was not a doctor – Adam was the physician.

"That's not our problem," he ranted.

"She says she's your daughter, but I think she mixed you up with a neighbour. You said at least three of our neighbours are doctors."

A curse, a pause, and a sigh arose from the other end of the cellphone line. "Go ask her if this is about tuition."

A realization, which explained puzzles and mysteries Jordan nurtured in the past about Adam, flooded his mind with plausible explanations, as he went to speak with the seemingly distressed young woman again. He was ready to blurt a question, when he stopped himself, thinking he should chose his words carefully. He also put the smartphone on speakerphone, so Adam could overhear their conversation. "I'm not talking to you," she said.

The young woman was mostly stoic, but her voice sounded even more morose, robotic. Jordan wondered what was wrong, and if she had injured herself with the bike lock. Stoic wasn't the right word to describe her demeanor, he thought, wondering how best to describe her to Adam. She seemed like the saddest person he ever saw or met in his life—she almost seemed as mournful as he remembered himself, not at his worst, but still mildly depressed.

"Is this about tuition?" he asked.

"Partly," she said.

"Could you elaborate, please."

"I am not talking to you."

"Okay, that's not the first time that I heard you say that."

Jordan returned to the smartphone, which he placed on speakerphone, so Adam didn't think it was a ruse. "Did you hear what she said? 'Partly?'"

Adam replied he would cancel the remainder of his afternoon and evening appointments. He drove his burgundy BMW straight home from the hospital on University Avenue. Now Jordan started to wonder and worry. Having realized his plans to register at the college that morning were nixed, he tried to make small talk with the young woman with the shaved head in black denim, a style he actually liked but eschewed for the conservatism of Adam, who favored polished shoes and suits and ties, but she truly wasn't interested in speaking with him. He tried to make certain if she was all right, and, fretting and hemming and hawing over her, he tried to make small talk with her.

When she became nasty and verbally abusive, cursing and hurtling insults in her muted, mechanical voice, he started to bake oatmeal muffins, which he enriched with protein powder, cooking and baking being a hobby he embraced after he entered into a domestic partnership with Adam, at a time when he didn't like to bake and cook, and was incompetent and clumsy in the kitchen. The baked goodies he hoped to feed the young woman somehow. Even though she insisted she didn't want to talk with him, and spoke to him like a robot, in this wooden manner which he found mysterious and exotic, he decided he would speak to her nonetheless, since he started to worry about her well-being, as she seemed intelligent, but also incredibly morose. Adam said this performance was exactly the sort of stunt one of his friends from his boogie nights in art college would have pulled. Then he asked her if she was an art college student, and she replied, "How do you know?"

Jordan thought that was the most naïve question and answer he heard in sometime. He thought they found an opening, found common ground, but then she quickly clammed up. Within the hour, while he baked and tried to make small talk and conversation with the young woman, Adam arrived.

Jordan was surprised the drive took underneath an hour, but Adam was energized by anger. The young woman and Adam acted with more than an inkling of familiarity. He told the young woman he had enough of this prank—

"It's not a prank."

"Ok. This performance art."

"It's not performance art."

Jordan could hear the pair arguing over a key for the bike lock, which she insisted she lost, tossed away, swallowed—Jordan didn't know which version to believe. While Adam tried to check her pockets, she bit his hand, and he reacted, slapping her face, cuffing her hands. When he discovered an empty pill bottle for phenelzine in her jacket pocket, he asked her where the rest of the medication was since she still had two weeks left on the prescription. She shook her head and refused to answer. "I need to know. Did you swallow all these Nardil tablets?" She looked away, gazed at the ground, and closed her eyes and clamped shut her mouth. Jordan could not stand to watch the domestic strife, so he stepped into the living room where he still couldn't resist watching their dispute. He ended up watching them fighting without the sound from the insulated picture window of the living room.

As Adam entered the house through the front door, he said, "We need a bike thief."

Despite the excitement, he noticed the young woman, including her back and the side of her head resting against the driver's door of the Tesla, appeared to have fallen asleep, with her neck wrapped, encircled, by the bike lock.

"You stressed her out. She suddenly became very animated, I noticed, when she started talking to you," Jordan said.

"The bitch," Adam gasped.

"She seems incredibly sad," Jordan said.

"She's always sad. She feeds off her own misery; she has undiagnosed borderline personality disorder."

"I thought you didn't believe in personality disorders. You told me you never made a single diagnosis of personality disorder in your entire career."

"I'm not a psychologist! But she thrives on misery—that's her modus operandi. If she wasn't suffering, she wouldn't be happy or have some sense of direction in life. She ends up spreading her dysphoria everywhere she goes."

"You didn't tell me you had a daughter."

"It's complicated."

"It's complicated? For heaven's sake—we're supposed to be getting married and you don't tell me you had a daughter in some previous secret life."

"It wasn't a previous secret life; it was just complicated. I was gay, and didn't know I was gay, and she was a lesbian, and she didn't know, either."

"You mean you were both bisexuals—I think that's what you're trying to say. You're the smarter one in this partnership, you could have figured out that part. But I don't blame you—it took me a life sentence to figure out I was gay, but you have lost credibility with me."

"We both couldn't figure it out, and we fucked because we had no one else."

"I didn't make the beast with two backs with anyone who came my way. In fact, I didn't fuck anyone, and I guess I'm still a virgin by conventional homophobic standards. I don't know if I should believe you."

"You have to believe. She finally discovered she was a lesbian, and she hated me afterwards—like everybody who has ever been in a relationship with me."

"Oh, now I'm supposed to believe everybody hates you." Shaking his head, Adam clamped his hand over his eyes in mental anguish. "Now this is supposed to be a pity party while the young lady outside has her neck in a bike lock attached to your electric car like a suicide bomber. She's in danger of injury, electrocution, suffocation—don't you think? But you dare tell me you're suddenly a father to a grown daughter so close to the date we're supposed to be married?"

Adam threw down his smartphone. "We need a bike thief!"

"I said we needed a bike thief and you corrected me. We need a bike mechanic. You're the genius: where do we find a bike mechanic?"

"At a bike repair shop. The question should be: can we find someone who can remove a bike lock at 7 pm."

"You're the guy with all the money. Money talks, everything else rides a bike."

Saying he knew a bike shop on Queen Street West, Adam decided he would quickly drive downtown before the store closed. He wanted Jordan to join him, but Jordan replied indignantly he should stay to monitor the condition of the young woman, even though he had no training of any type of credentials as first responder or healthcare worker. Earlier, complaining he didn't even know CPR or the Heimlich maneuver, Adam urged him to enrol in a weekend Red Cross or First Aid program. Jordan again approached Frida and tried to offer her some solace and consolation, but she continued to insist she didn't want to talk to him. Then Jordan vacuumed the living room, dusted the coffee tables and widescreen television, and cleaned and polished the windows while he watched Frida from the living room picture window. Then, when he saw she lost consciousness, he went outside and checked on her condition. Jordan checked for the pulses in her neck and wrists, but they appeared thready, weak. He gasped in relief when he saw she appeared to be breathing. Still, out of concern and worry, he called Adam on the smartphone. On Spadina Avenue near Bloor Street,

Adam squealed to a stop for a takeout slice of pizza at his favorite pizza restaurant, which he said was genuinely Italian and therefore better tasting.

"Why are you wasting my time? Did you ever think she might be asleep?"

"Yes, but she is shackled to a bike lock."

"What do you expect? She's been crucifying herself there for—how long?"

"All day, I guess, but there's also bruising on her neck."

"You probably didn't notice it before. I did encourage you to call the police."

"You want to call the police on your own daughter? Why don't I call an ambulance, instead?"

"Sure, call an ambulance, but, as soon as you explain the situation, the dispatcher will probably end up summoning the police as well. And that's fine by me."

After Jordan turned on the speakerphone, the couple ended up practically shouting at each other over smartphones. "Listen, calm down, and I'll be there with the bike mechanic within the hour."

After Adam hung up his smartphone and finished wolfing down his pizza slice, he spotted the young man, with a shaved head, and plenty of tattoos, which he noticed because he wore no shirt, outside the pizza restaurant. The shirtless man accosted one of the Uber Eats driver guarding a pair of e-bikes he and his fellow delivery person locked to the utility pole and bike stand on the boulevard outside the restaurant patio. He asked the Uber Eats delivery person, a diminutive man, if he was a rat. Thinking a drug deal had gone awry, Adam feared he would witness the young man, his head shaved, pull out a handgun and shoot wildly in an ambush. Instead, the interlocutor brandished a rechargeable portable grinder and cut the bike lock away from the delivery person's e-bike.

Adam intervened and told the fellow he would make it worth his while if he helped him with his own bike lock.

After Adam played The Clash on his BMW compact disc player, Sid said he played in a rock band, which covered Clash hits and played at The Horsehoe Tavern and The Bovine Sex Club. Adam bonded with Sid over punk rock music. Within the hour, the BMW lurched to a stop in their driveway. Sid stepped out of the passenger door with hesitation and trepidation as Adam introduced him.

Sid grew exasperated at cutting a bike lock near the neck of the young woman, but Adam encouraged him to press ahead with the task. Wincing in pain, Jordan couldn't witness the proceeding and returned to the house. After Adam covered Frida's face with his leather bomber jacket, the bike thief grudgingly took the small portable grinder to the bike lock. When the battery charger suddenly died, Sid cursed. He insisted he wanted to leave. Sid, wanting nothing to do with an unconscious girl shackled to a car door handle, grew afraid. He told Adam to find someone else to do his dirty work. But Adam argued with Sid, insisted he finish the job, and offered to pay him more.

While Jordan winced and looked away from the scene, shifting in his new position at the picture window, Adam gripped his daughter's head and protected her face and neck with the jacket. Sid hammered the bike lock with steady, forceful blows, until he broke clean through the remainder of the U bolt and bar. Sid stood back from Adam, as he tried to explain to him that Adam was a doctor, but he merely held up his open hands and gestured to him to back off while he made a telephone call for an ambulance. When the police arrived in the wake of the paramedics, Sid drifted off down the street.

After they followed behind the ambulance in the Tesla, they were both interviewed, in the emergency department of the hospital, by the police officers and a detective, as Frida remained in a comatose state.

"Shouldn't we call her mother?" Jordan asked.

"Her mother died years ago," Adam replied. "She overdosed—probably committed suicide. She was another starving artist."

"Starving artist—what is this fetish you have with starving artists? What are you trying to insinuate?"

"I'm not insinuating anything. Just stating bald facts."

"What is it about you and artists, anyway?"

"Are you serious?"

"Your wife was an artist, your artist is an artist, I was an artist," Jordan said.

"She wasn't really a wife, and did you ever think I might love good art and appreciate those who produce it?"

Jordan grunted and bought a takeout coffee, Irish Cream flavored, from the kiosk near the hospital entrance and stepped onto University Avenue. Worried he had grown distant and aloof, Adam followed him.

"I just want out," Adam said curtly.

"What?"

"I'm ready to walk down University Avenue—you know like a 'Free Man in Paris'— and take the next subway train out of your life."

"Well, you're certainly not taking my Telsa!"

"I'm serious!" Jordan hissed. "I'll find a room in the Humber College dorm and start school for X-Ray technician, or even interior decorator."

"And who will pay for tuition, texts, and rent?"

Jordan had reached a threshold, as Adam had gone over the line. Deciding to escape this astonishing and unexpected predicament, he decided to take the next flight from Pearson International Airport to the city near his hometown and another flight, a connecting flight. Down the street from the hospital on university avenue, Jordan took the subway to Kipling station. Then he rode an express bus for the long, droning voyage along streets and expressways to the airport. He bought a ticket from the airline service counter. His smartphone, which he wanted to return in one final dramatic gesture to Adam but forgot, rang.

"Jordie, she's dead. I need you. Help."

Jordan remembered the formal traditional wedding vows he wanted, which Adam nixed when they planned their marriage. The simple, basic words in the vows haunted him: "for better, for worse, for richer, for poorer, in sickness and in health."

Jordan took the next express bus to Kipling subway station and rode the commuter train to the station near hospital. He was greeted in the emergency department waiting room by Adam sobbing. The doctor, friends with Adam from their glory days as students at The University of Toronto medical school, said Frida was still alive, by virtue of the fact there was still electrical activity in her brain. In the end, Frida was not expected to recover. So the doctor needed a decision as to whether she should disconnect the life support. The doctor took Jordan aside, to a part of the emergency department, where he felt his anxiety grow, his palms sweat, his heart thump in foreboding, as he saw several nurses monitoring the progress of patients attached to heart monitors. Adam consulted with his doctor friend and gave her the message he was deferring to Jordan for a final decision on questions of Frida's life and death.

"Adam wants me to decide if we should disconnect his daughter from life support?"

The emergency doctor nodded, and Jordan thought, in a sense, this might be construed as emotional manipulation, but with that pronouncement he decided he would stay. For several more long emotionally agonising days Frida lived, unconscious, in a coma, moderate according to the Glasgow coma scale. He was Catholic, and he would not allow the young woman to die, not on his watch.

Several days later, as the couple camped out in the hospital, the only sigh of life she provided was minor sparks of electricity in her brain. The doctor assured and reassured him she was "cognitively a vegetable," at which point he made the fateful decision. In an emotional encounter in the cafeteria Adam backed him up. After Frida passed, Adam broke down, saying goodbyes at her bedside in the intensive care unit, his grief expressed in loud sobs and cries.

When the couple left the hospital, they abandoned his Tesla electric car in a glorified underground parking lot downtown. Late through the night and early in the morning, they hiked northwards across Toronto, taking a marathon walk across Toronto through the beautiful summer night, hot, humid.

They stopped for takeout coffee at twenty-four-hour Tim Horton's on Yonge Street, near Eglinton Avenue. Adam tried to reassure him they didn't accidentally kill his daughter; her blood samples revealed she had a toxic level of the MAO antidepressant Phelzine in her bloodstream, which, Adam said, the empty prescription bottle explained. She took the old school antidepressant because it was the only medication her psychiatrist found effective for her condition. But Jordan wasn't so confident; he was familiar with antidepressants and had taken plenty of them, including in overdoses. He wondered if the bottle could have contained enough pills to cause her demise, but after he commented vaguely to that effect they walked in silence. The only person they saw during that marathon walk, whom they recognized amidst the nightlife and the urban stragglers, few and far between, was Sid.

Adam shouted after him, but Sid merely ignored his abrupt high-spirited antics. The bike thief took his portable cordless electric grinder to the bike lock securing a mountain bicycle parked outside a fast-food restaurant on midtown Yonge Street. Adam and Jordan arrived home as the orange sun rose through a misty horizon, smoky and obscured by fog, as one neighbour trundled their garbage and recyclables to the curb and another neighbour drove along the idyllic street with his coffee in a sippy cup on the roof of his car.

# Gambling

By Robert Cooperman

At the track, unless you have inside information—
like the gangster father of a teenage friend—
you're doomed to lose.  I knew a guy who studied

the racing form like the Talmud, clocked morning workouts;
when I asked how he did, he confessed he kept his losses
to five percent a year, and if not for his post office job

he'd be broke as a squeegee guy on the Bowery.
Bored one Saturday, two friends and I drove
to Belmont and basked in the stands in the sun;

we bet a few bucks on some races, lost them all,
and on the way home, my car blew a tire
on the Belt Parkway.  If not for Steve's skill

with a jack and lug nuts, that car would still be sitting,
crippled on the shoulder: a horse that came up lame
in a claiming race: the end of my gambling career,

except for one morning of reading the point spread
on NBA games; at one, I rubbed my eyes, knowing
in my bones the home team couldn't cover the spread,

and mentioned that to Beth.  "Know a bookie?"
"No," I replied, but Jeff does." "Call him." I didn't.
I got the line right, but God forbid, what slippery path

that one lucky stab might've led me down.

# Reboot

By Mark A. Fisher

walking outside again
down empty streets
looking past dusty cars
and the memories of bars
and restaurants
left unvisited
while hints of echos
laugh in the lonely parks
without a vaccine against
stupidity likely this year
the virus in our operating system
traps our reboot
in an infinite ransomware loop
our constitutional anti-viral
cannot seem to stop
so it's just gonna be
one of those dystopian games
where everyone has already lost

# Pandemic Prognosis

By Carl "Papa" Palmer


I went to Lowes yesterday

wore my mask

stayed six feet apart

this morning my throat hurts

my chest feels tight

do I have a cough?

a sense of smell?

a fever? COVID?

should I call 9-1-1?

stay in the bathroom

not to infect my wife?

I hear from the kitchen,

Breakfast is ready.

False Alarm,

I smell bacon.

# Untitled

By Derek Roper

# Revelation 1:3

By Mike L. Nichols

Humanity was saved by the next plague.
The gluttonous use of resources ceased.
Humans huddle dirty in their dark family
enclaves and recall meaningless bygone things:

Packed tight second lane from the right
rolling home at ten MPH to
Binge watching streaming TV.
Tonguing the clotted orange
Cheeto dust from all five fingers.
Consider buying bigger jeans.
Believing that we are the center of the universe.
Thinking God loves us.

Recall the faces of the dead.
Invite them into this dancing circle
of candlelight. Unafraid, because the dead carry
no disease – only glad tidings.

# Leaving

By Lee Ellis

I stagger
    to sea,
the gulf between us—
    vast waters
        hushed.

Your words, spiteful north winds,
    blow my heat to shivers.

From the shell-dappled drift line,
    I throw my bruises to the
        ripples where one-legged statuettes sleep.

Lost in your distant,
aching in your sullen,
    I test the sand at my feet,
        grains of regret
            sifting free.

I leave your landlocked,
    iron heart
        barnacle encrusted, scarred,
            and bloodless

Arms hanging as broken wings,
    hands brined
        and insubstantial as sea foam,
    I slip into the biting flow,
        breath stolen in a deep trough.

# El Medano Montana

By CJP Lee

# Covid Virus. . . a modern Minotaur

By Jeanette Willert

In the follies
of the Greek Gods
we find, yet, ourselves.

As a corona virus
attacks and kills
with bestial efficiency,
we consider
the labyrinth
we are consigned to
& the miniscule Minotaur
marauding our organs,
murdering at will
as it charges
our corridors
and trashes
our chambers.

No ball of thread
will deliver us
from you, brute;
no Theseus
will lay you low.
It will take
a Pasteur or Salk
white-coated,
test-tube savvy
to slay you,
brazen bull

# Wash Your Hands!

By Faruk Buzhala

When you think you've lied
Wash your hands
When you think you've slandered
Wash your hands
When you think you've intrigued
Wash your hands
When you think you've cheated
Wash your hands
When you think you've abused
Wash your hands
When you think you've misinterpreted
Wash your hands
When you think you've misused it
Wash your hands
When you think you've betrayed
Wash your hands
When you think you've hurt
Wash your hands!

P.S.
Even Pontius Pilate washed his hands saying:
hopefully the coronavirus doesn't bug me!"

# Empty Spaces

By Jaina Cipriano

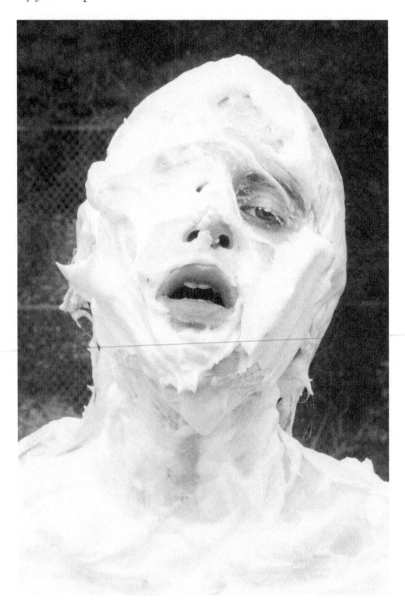

# Mask Time

By Faruk Buzhala

We wear masks to shut-up our mouths!
Our lips remains non visible under them,
Our teeth are not visible too,
Even the smile remains not a hidden secret,
The bad smell too,
And the words we speak are not well articulated, with no
regret.

We do wear the masks to prevent the virus from entering in
us,
And versa, not letting go out from ourselves.

We do wear mask over our face-mask,
The lipstick in women's lips remains unseen,
Same with botox in their swelled lips,
Can't feel even the breath.

We wear original mask to cover the fakeness in this pandemic
time,
we follow the advices from the responsible institutions
How to care about ourselves and the other,
Although, most of us do not follow them.

We do wear masks while we walk in the streets and
When we see a familiar face,
We take off the mask to greet them, as sign of respect!

## Weather Forecast

By Carl "Papa" Palmer

Looking like a usual foggy summer morning

of our Puget South town just south of Seattle,

normally burning off to sunshine before noon,

but this is smoke from the fires in California.

Air quality level shows us worst in the world,

no protection provided by corona virus masks

as we pray for a rain to wash them both away.

# Okay, Now Read the Bottom Line for Me

By Mike L. Nichols

We never saw it coming with our
pupils like pinpricks in response
to the deluge of consumerism.
When the American façade
failed, forcing dilation like
a heartless optometrist,
it was too late.

'Merica the serfdom snapped
open her eyes, came full awake.

# The Fox

By Emily Bilman

In the bus, people spoke about Covid-19.
Like swarms of sardines swirling round
And round the black-blue shadow
Of the sea to reach the light, I imagined
Distant queues gathering in check-outs
Before gaining the daylight outside.
In the bus, adolescents chatted about
Masquerades, giggled, and laughed.
Then, unexpectedly, we heard the screeching
Brakes as the bus halted in the middle
Of a natural reserve. Through the large
Windows we saw a majestic red fox
With a fur of amber gold crossing the strait
Road in the wan winter light, its torso
And long bushy tail all tainted in white;
Its pointed ears and taut snout all alert.
Animals that keep a sylvan vigil in the forest
Move, hide, and hunt, sometimes uncloak
Themselves warily. Separated by a verge
From the bland gray asphalt road it traversed,
The guileful and shrewd eyes of the fox shone
Like children's agate marbles vying
To target other marbles. All along,
I scrutinized the fox's heedful steps
As it entered the dark green fir forest
Uplifted before us as an alpine totem
Which we neglected until the virus hit us.

# Whine

By Dee Allen


One of the most annoying things

I've heard of late

Was caught one morning whilst riding

A B.A.R.T.* subway train from Oakland to S.F.


Some lady in sunglasses boarded

And took a seat eight paces from mine,

Complained to her friend on a Smartphone

About how she couldn't wait for


Everything to be restored

Back to normal.


What was considered

Normal

Before the Pandemic


Did damage

To certain

Races, classes, sexes, sexualities,

Abilities and nationalities

Of people, species
Of animals and this
Nurturing old Earth
Herself.

I don't want a
Return to the old ways,
To methods of mayhem. I want to see change
For the better, after this global sickness subsides.

So you want things
Back to normal, huh?
Got any cheese and crackers
To go with that whine?

W: 7.16.2020
*Bay Area Rapid Transit.

# Normalcy in Chaos

By Carl Papa Palmer

hearing her harping
on all that's changed
since the virus struck
makes me appreciate
that she hasn't

# Now

By Mark Fisher

there ain't no barbarians
at the our gates
'cause they seem
to want to move away
from this our
beautiful
bullied
and burned
California
to cross some
barely fettered
timezone systematic
madness
to reach their own
utopia in Kansas
or Oklahoma
already impoverished
by their dreams

## Static

By RP Verlaine

**The**
Shivering
In winter
**deafening silence of floors**
Only
The
Cigarette
Burns.
**absent footsteps**
**of ghosts.**

# Lonesome #1

By B.A. Brittingham

# Afraid

By Mark Fisher

I've dropped into some odd

Twilight Zone episode

of a mad little village

playing metaphor

for a whole country

as little boys get bandaged

after fights beneath stars

debased by the change

of not looking up

as they fail to see

that fear has made them

into monsters

# Corona Virus

By Sumati Muniandy

Finally, the corona virus revealed how miserable you are,
How ugly you feel being with yourself,
You are scared of your own being,
Isolation had been fearful.

You can't accept aloneness,
You panic being alone.
Ridiculous!

Parents complain their children are bored at home,
No park, no playground, no school, no tuition,
They are restless!

We never learn, neither we teach our children to be alone,
Aloneness is beauty,
This is the state when you spend time with yourself.
You get the chance to analyse things and know what is wrong
and right.
You talk to your inner being,

# Chicago #26

By B.A. Brittingham

# Like Cockroaches, Hit the Lights and See Them Scuttle.

By Mike L. Nichols

Along the lane where crocuses are

no longer groomed, children run,

fast as ever they can, from

overfed men in night optics

and body armor. Malformed

and weak with hunger, she always

was the slowest of us. The fear unfolding

in my chest stopped me turning to take

her hand. Safe behind the rubble,

we made eye contact while the

guns of broad shouldered men spread

blooms across her chest.

# Rolling Out

By Dee Allen

"DUE TO THE ELECTION
VICTORY OF OPPONENT
JOE BIDEN, OUR PRESIDENT'S
STAND-BY ORDER HAS BEEN RESCINDED.

WE'RE ROLLING OUT."

Rolling out
To save Western Civilisation—
They love to blow
On that dog whistle

Rolling out
To prevent White genocide—
They obviously
Don't read statistics

Rolling out
For the Whites who built Western society alone—
They obviously
Forsaken the slaves who raised up wood, mortar &
stone

Rolling out

To give multi-cultural populace

Their own racial reckoning

For the loss of a "fearless leader"


Rolling out

To keep America great—

On the streets like no other—

Maybe Hitler's Brownshirts* and Nazi skinhead gangs


Rolling out

With American flags in their horde—

Proud to sow intimidation, reap domestic terror

Quasi-military boys so proud to be so damn wrong—


W: Thankstaking 2020

*Das Sturmabteilung [ SA – "Storm Unit" ].

# Charon LLC

By JBMulligan

The Gods were human. Everybody knew that. Charon, whose mother was Nyx, who frightened Zeus himself, was well aware of this. Charon had seen the big bad King of the Gods stomping and muttering outside the cave where Nyx sheltered Charon's brother, Hypnos, while Hypnos peered from behind his mother's skirt, and mouthed and muttered the same sort of threats and curses that Zeus did. Charon had seen the moonless dark in his mother's eyes as she stared out at Zeus, who, after all his posturing, turned and walked away, kicking over a large oak in his impotent anger.

Nyx found out was her son had done to anger the God, and Hypnos had really gotten his ass whipped over that one, pleasing Charon like an unexpected present – "You tried to put him to sleep?" she had shouted. But the beating had come from their mother, not Zeus. Charon sometimes thought perhaps that is why Zeus didn't much like him.

Charon had been given the job of ferrying the dead by somebody who had not bothered to ask if he was interested in doing that for a day, or a year, or all of time. He hadn't really wanted the job, but when the collecting of the coins had been explained, he thought he could get used to it. There were worse jobs, and he did like the river's rippling skin and the shiver of fish like flames just beneath the surface, and the way that the water never thought or stopped. Charon would have rather been the river than a boatman, but such was life, even among the immortals.

The traffic had been a slow and steady flow for many centuries, broken occasionally by a sudden flood of the famine-stricken or the war-torn. Ares sometimes watched from a distance as a particularly choice mortal clambered onto the ferry, and Charon could never tell if the God was pleased or sad by the passage of this particular one of his victims.

The dead of war hardly ever had coins for the passage, so were forced to spend one hundred years pacing on the riverbank. Far more of the famine victims actually were able to pay than you would think. Charon was never sure what that meant.

As the mass of humans began to grow, the tide of the dead gradually increased, and the storms of war and disaster were larger, and sometimes, Charon would have to keep the newly dead waiting far longer than he would like, especially as many of them tended to grumble about why you had to pay a coin when you were forced to wait. The ferryman would explain caustically that the coin bought you a passage, not a set time of departure or arrival. This led to prolonged discussions with people whom Charon would never see again, and he found he had much better, and shorter, conversations being understanding and even apologetic. And so, Charon discovered the First Principle of Customer Service: a satisfied customer is a quiet customer.

Eventually, Charon decided to add a second ferry, which naturally required a second ferryman. This turned out, after several failed apprentices, to be a fellow aptly named Dim. The kid couldn't figure out what water was, if he fell out of the boat. But he had a strong back and arms, and he followed simple instructions quite well, since he wasn't bright enough to work out any alternatives. Also, he was wonderfully patient with the customers, and especially good with children.

Ferrying children never bothered Charon, since he imagined that they arrived at some splendid playground of toys and trees and fun. Then again, Charon made sure never to ask what happened to any of his passengers, once they got off the boat and shivered beneath Hades' boney smile.

As the living population continued to increase, it became necessary to add a third ferry, and then a fourth. The deluge of the dead during bad times was indescribable, and Charon was never really sure how he or any of his workers survived. The new hires were, unsurprisingly, brighter than

200

Dim, so training them went pretty quickly. After that, he found himself, more and more, on the shore directing the milling traffic, assuring people that things would be fine, that yes, there were enough boats, and no, he'd never been to the Underworld, so didn't actually know what it was like. Those were the sensible questions. It amazed him that some people had managed to survive at all, as stupid as they were. But he kept on smiling.

Eventually, Charon had to give up life on the river completely, and take care of things on the shore, such as scheduling, and complaining workers who apparently imagined they were customers. He gave up his rustic clothing and his scraggly beard when he found out that people were more cooperative when he gave off an air of officialdom and order.

Of course, lawyers were forever on their way to the Underworld: there was a rumor that there was one lawyer in the Elysian Fields, but Charon found that impossible to imagine. And despite an absence of any court with jurisdiction over the River Lethe or any business or conveyance on or adjacent to it – well, attorneys were attorneys, and not nearly as human as Gods, and it was useless to try to drown the dead, so Charon pulled aside an attorney who was, astonishingly, without a coin for passage, and came to an agreement.

The answer, it seems, was in a Limited Liability Corporation. This protected Charon and his workers, who were pretty decent sorts, from the more obnoxious attorneys. Were there less obnoxious attorneys? At any rate, papers were drawn up and signed, and the attorney and Charon were both quite pleased with the results.

Sometimes, Charon would look out at his fleet gliding efficiently across the wine-dark river, watching the light spangle off the water like spilled coins, and he longed for the old days, the original days. Whoever the God of Improvements was, people needed to sacrifice more.

# Bad Governance (Prosey Poems)

By Anagha Joy

## 1
### The Rag -Sweep
He seemed
only 8 years old.
At his age,

I was at school trying to memorize
things that held no meaning for me.

When I asked him his name
he articulated only sound
the little rag sweep boy.

Diptty-Dap
Dippty-Dap
Chugged the 126 up train.

At 8:00 p.m
The Little One
was still sweeping the floor
of the compartment
littered by my prosperity.

Diptty-Dap
Dippty-Dap
Chugged the 126 up train
taking the little one
away
from his house.

At 9:00p.m
The Little rag-sweep
had finished his collection

and huddled himself to sleep

in a corner of the compartment.

Diptty-Dap
Dippty-Dap
Chugged the 126 up train.
Three days back
he was on the 125 Down train
earning his livelihood.

Toys and school he had none
Only the floor of the compartment
filled with the litter of my prosperity.

Diptty-Dap
Dippty-Dap
Chugged
the 126 and 125
carrying
the rag-sweep boy
In a whorl for existence.

## 2
## HONOUR- KILLING

Love is built up in abundance;
gestures of love reserve strong support;
all this for mankind.

Bewitched in Love - two bodies with a single soul:
the heart brews richer and flutters in joy.

Love is not the communion of two bodies:
but more than two bodies merging as one,
an intervention of a nation's culture, tradition and societal
norm
Of Caste, Creed, Religion, Community......


Uninterrupted Powers,
Traversing the path of transparent death
In the name of 'Honor Killing'.

My heart thudding with erections of anger
echoing a whisper, a voice in my he:
'LOVE IS DEAD
KINDNESS IS DEAD
HUMANITY IS DEAD'.

Tempering my hot young blood,
Soothing my fuming heart in anger -
All this would erupt as a burning inferno in a person without
LOVE, KIDNESS and HUMANITY and reduce to ashes.

Catechize
Why? Why?
Why lash the tender heart of the young lad and the lass
?

Why? Why?
Framework of society are are bars of brutality.


Please! Please!
A humble request from a humble soul
Let's make this world a better place to explore, learn and
importantly to LIVE and LOVE .

# 3

## 73 Years of Freedom

When I was a brat

And in school,

My history teacher

Told me of a man by name,

Mohandas Karamchand Gandhi

Otherwise, known as the Mahatma.

He told us of his spirited fight

Against

The enslaver of my father and grandfather.


He told us

Of thousands,

Who hearkened

To the call for freedom,

And the thousands

Who suffered for a free country.

I was born in 1994

The year is now 2020

And I am 26 years old

Freedom is a word

That has meaning

Only for an intellectual

Or for a moneyed man.

Yes,

My sisters

Have been sold for money


And

My brother

Pick thrash out of dustbins

And have territorial wars

With squads of dogs

For a morsel of food.

When I write this

I am in an air-conditioned room,

But

My mother with blistered feet

And a rasping throat,

In a dehydrated frame,

Is scratching the wastelands

For a handful of water.

**4**

## GREAT DESTRUCTION
(4 Aug 2020 5:45pm)

The wind howls in the heaven:
There are no trees to bend to the lash of the stinging air.
The sound streams through the buildings,
Bring in its wake – a dreary sign of a great destruction.

The clouds in the heaven are in a ferment:
black clouds joining up to each other- the store houses of the
heavens are in pain:
And in a rush of events the earth erupts with bursts of fire.

The earth reverberated:
    The shreaks,
      The sorrow,
      The sadness,
      The wailing:
There were no ends to the tears and the wails.

    Seven storey buildings,
      Six storey buildings,
      Five storey buildings:
    all collapsed in a heap to ground level:
The rubble making small mounts of concrete and steel,
And creating a millions of homeless people:
Enshrouding the wealth of the building owners,
And an innumerable number of people buried in the rubble.

    Seven days,
      Night and day,
    They cleared the rubble:
A few human beings we're extracted alive but wounded,
And after seven days they gave up as there was nothing more
to do.

# Immortality of Mortality

By Yeshi Choden

The return of the twitch in my left eye

promises the continuity of an old glory

and the grasp on some sense of identity

I thought was lost, is thus revived

if caprice numbs, it also moves


I stand opposite a face, whole from all

the holes and for a heartbeat

I recognize it as my own

I am fond of mirrors and all the reflections

I see or sometimes don't see because sometimes

it's just glass and that too I love


always find me over the line

between what is felt and what said

looking to sing my way through the confusion

and toward liberation, find me there

from what, liberation from what?

whatever hurts, nay, what haunts


questions without answers, I have got

too many of those but answers, when I

make, I make and leave them

on the tip of my tongue to melt and make

me bitter.

Its like cough syrup

only good for when you have a cough


if there walks a special calm through me

in steps louder than solitude

followed by echoes of sentences I forsook

in times of gentle apathy

that is my cue

I am to listen

# The Best Teacher

By Jeffrey G. Delfin

Considered as our second parent
Our guiding light in every moment
No matter what path we are going to take
I am sure that you will be there for our sake

You are the source of our knowledge
Motivates us to have some courage
You make us strong when we are about to fall
You raise us up to help us conquer our fears once in for all

You shape our minds to be a great leader;
remind us the that to be a leader, first, we have to be a good
follower,
You taught us to be a role model to others,
We should amplify the goodness in our hearts;
treat every person as our brothers

You said that respecting other people is a good gesture;
we should respect each others' culture,
In time we will be harvesting the seeds of kindness,
That will grow in the hearts of everyone with gladness

Sometimes aside from being a teacher and a parent,

You can transform as a friend who can give his arms to give us
strength,
We can face the challenges in life as easy and possible,
Because you serve us our shield to protect us in times of trouble

I remember one time when I was in anguish,
I failed in one of my subjects; hoping the sadness inside me will
vanquish
You told me that in life we will be facing different problems and
consequences
You stood by me and said that I have to face my failure and be
brave to gain my defenses

You are like my father who is hardworking
Even beyond office hours you are like a machine that is still
functioning
You want us to absorb new learning each in everyday,
I know you want us to be ready in every step of our way

I am so glad that I met you along the way,
Living in this world makes us happy and okay
You, my teacher, is always there for me
Listening to everything that I say, you always bring out the best
that I can be

For you my teacher, patience is truly a virtue
You wait for us to grow, to be mature, to be honest and to be true

It is not only knowledge that you have imparted

But as well as values that we can share to people wholehearted


Without a doubt you serve as an inspiration

To pursue our dreams and achieve our life's ambition

You are a teacher, a parent, a sibling, a friend rolled into one

I guess it will be hard for us to be like you, a superhuman


I hope and I pray that you may live longer,

Longer enough to spread your wisdom especially those who are in hunger,

I know you can feed them with knowledge, skills, courage, and virtue every day

To survive this so-called life and be able to be a catalyst of change to the learners of today

# Anamnesis

By Dr. Shubha Dwivedi

What you taught me
Was only the half truth
Now looking for the remaining truth of the matter
I question and verify the veritable facts
That were handed down to me
By the previous generation academics and scholars
I remember of having been told
that the archetypes for women
Were no other than
Draupadi, Sita, Shakuntala, Savitri
Who lived in the shadows of their counterparts?
Whose existence was made conspicuous by their
obsequiousness
Who faltered and failed in their roles as women?
Yet reached the pinnacle of womanhood
With their services and submission
Through execution of duties and deference to the
unbreakable code.
Kunti, Gandhari,
Amba, Madhavi, Hidimba
Endowed with intellect and grace
They remained an enigma for the people of their age
 And succumbed to servility without showing their rage
Living in the present-day world
I wonder what they had wanted
For themselves
Love of home and hearth
Or some simple pleasures of the world
Or just a will to subvert the stereotype

What were the echoing sounds behind their sobs and
snuffles?
Wish they could cry their heart out
And speak up their mind.
In a world submerged in *Adharma*
They epitomized virtue and uprightness-
Sins that brought eternal damnation
For the female in generations thereafter
Wish they had known
That the truth was delusional like the archetypal golden Deer
or Marichika
That the man-made world was
An ornamented gold gilt pot,
covered with a lid
What lay underneath
Was a story full of secrets,
riddles and mysteries
Reeking with blood
Of the silent sufferers
Waiting to be redeemed.

# No More Rank And File

By Linda Imbler

The constant sway
of genuine concern
charms your heart as
you arrive in the middle.
It takes form in your breast
as you view each person as one of
indeterminate status.

# December

By Jenn Powers

# Precipice

By Dee Allen

Gladly say goodbye
To the proven nightmare,
These past
Four years—

The precipice
On which I stand
Is crowded with
The eager

Waiting on
Cures for
Both viruses.
The one
Ailing bodies,
The one
Extinguishing love.

Smooth transition
Into another era,
Focus of everybody's
Endogenic wishes, appealing even to my jaded self.

When I close my eyes,
I hear the popular song of

"What Now?"

W: 11.23.2020

# The Mind

By A Whittenberg

Is

As fragile as

The dream

It dreams

The black voice

# For The New Term

By Dave Medd

The kids are back today, faces in sets
like cigarette cards (footballers or beauties)
collecting lessons on gods.
Yesterday was planning and agendas;
tomorrow will be maths and mines and mums.

Some bring disillusion in new dresses,
blank limbs on desks, form to be filled in later.
We offer old man's vision,
skeletons, computers, winning tickets (maybe),
torn rags from last year's teacher's lexicon,

light from his failing star. Some wear only
mother's yellow hope, an old lace veil
shielding all but a blink of eyes
that long to see, when threadbare habits fail,
how God has blown out all her old curriculum.

# Child Warning

By CJP Lee

# Routine

By Matthew Kerr

**Put in some directors: What would Coppola or Scorcese or Kubrick think? Pull some film theory from the story I was writing. Adopt elements from that.**

**Also, blend in the Two Therapists ideas.**

**Imagining what the actors think of me. "What ifs"- imagining different scenarios.**

**Feeling powerless.**

My first short film was accepted into zero of the twenty three festivals it was entered into. There is no reason for me to think I am any good at making films.

I am misguided.

**EXT: PARKING LOT-DAY**

**A man wearing a black mask with a skull over his mouth and nose, sunglasses, hat, black gloves, as well as a one piece coverall uniform with the name TONY F stitched on it walks to his van carrying a cardboard box with shipping stickers on it. He opens the back and puts the box inside. He gets into the van which has a delivery decal on the back window (Uber, Lyft).**

**He gets behind the wheel, taps his phone, and drives away.**

***

We are living in times of great uncertainty. Life has changed dramatically due to the Coronavirus. Jobs have been lost, social isolation is taking its toll, frustration is threatening to boil over. Ugly creatures that, for periods of time lay dormant, have slithered their way to the surface of our society, our conscious minds, as they always do during upheavals in our "normal" routines: xenophobia, racism, sexism, etc. Maybe these pathologies have always been part of our normal routines and the pandemic has just exposed them.

Do I make a short film during all this?

When viewed in the context of the heroic work of healthcare workers and the Black Lives Matter protests and the number of people being hospitalized and dying and families being torn apart at the border, my project seems woefully trite and insignificant, Honestly, what does it matter if it gets done or not? Is the world going to miss out on some vital message if it doesn't get completed?

That is the problem with passion; it leaves you with no choice. Like it or not, this is my thing. Passion, true passion,

223

gives you tunnel vision; it robs you of rationality. It doesn't matter what else is going on or the issues or obstacles that always arise. It has got to get done.

And that is the magic of passion: it leaves you with no choice. If you are passionate about a project, you really don't have to put any effort into it; you just do it. It is as much a part of you as eating and breathing.

However, passion alone is not enough. There are always obstacles and a person needs to have the commitment to deal with them.

## INT: VAN-DAYNIGHT

**The delivery man drives the streets. We see the effects of the Coronavirus: people wearing masks, restaurants with tables outside, signs thanking workers, Black Lives Matter Signs, Back the Blue signs, Trump/Pence signs, Biden/Harris signs.**

**As he drives he listens to a podcast about the pandemic and the presidential campaign and the protests.**

In March of 2020, I was in pre-production for my short film, Authenticity, which was to be shot in July. The script is about a young woman of color who is trying to make a short film. She is smart and well-educated but has problems communicating her vision to the crew and the actors. She is trying to find her identity.

Then the Coronavirus reared its head; we were being told to wear masks and stay home. Public venues closed: restaurants, bars, gyms etc. Schools turned to remote learning. Gatherings of more than ten people were banned.

Lockdown. My timing really could not have been worse.

Throughout April and into May I held out hope that things might calm down and we could pull it off but, by the beginning of June it had become apparent that the project was not going to be feasible. It would be very difficult to get locations in which to shoot. Even if we could get a location, having 10-15 people in one space was going to be a problem. Obviously, when we were shooting, everyone would be in close proximity to each other; the actors would have to take their masks off and many people were going to be uncomfortable with that. We had put out a casting call and barely anyone responded which gave us a pretty clear indication that people just didn't want to be on set at that time. In addition, I'm sure that people were too preoccupied with their jobs and financial situations to think about acting in a short film.

I had worked hard on the script for Authenticity. It had gone through at least nine drafts and I was very proud and excited to shoot it. Now, the rug had been pulled out from under me. Since my job as a teacher had pretty much halted I had a lot of time to write a new script but it was hard to switch gears since I had invested so much time and energy into "Authenticity". I felt like I had lost all the energy and momentum that had been building over the previous few months.

**EXT. ROAD-DAY**
**The delivery van is driving the streets.**

The guitar virtuoso, Steve Vai, played with Frank Zappa, who is regarded as one of the greatest musical innovators of modern times. He said that Zappa would experiment with guitars, take them apart and rework them to get certain sounds that he wanted. Vai said that if Zappa ran into a situation where he couldn't get what he wanted, he would "absorb" the obstacle. He would try new designs and techniques to at least get something new, even if it wasn't quite what he had in mind.

Absorb the Obstacle: If you can't get over it, under it, around it or bulldoze your way through it, make it work for you. Absorb it like a sponge, make it take on a different form, like water cutting rock in the Grand Canyon.

It's not like I was the only one in this boat. Many people's creative plans had been derailed. A former student of mine, Liz Campanelli, is an actor and she sent me a link to a play she was in, *The Importance of Being Earnest*. She and her acting troupe had been in the midst of rehearsals when the pandemic hit and closed all the theaters so they were doing on Zoom. I have to say that the performance was tough to watch because the actors are all in different locations and there was no music and everything was static but the costumes and background looked great and the actors did a fine job delivering their lines. And, bottomline, they did it. They had absorbed the obstacle.

Maybe the Coronavirus, instead of being an obstacle, could be turned into an opportunity.

**INT. BASEMENT-DAY**
**We see a black backdrop with a spotlight shining on it, a stool with a bottle of water on it, and a microphone stand.**
**We hear off screen...**

**JEFF (VO)**
**All right everyone, give it up for Jeff Lydon!**

**JEFF LYDON, a forty six year old white male, bounds into the frame and waves. He begins doing his stand-up comedy routine**

**Jeff comes bounding into the frame.**

Jeff Lydon worked as an accountant before he quit his job in March to pursue his dream of being a comic. Before the pandemic hit he had performed at a few open mic events, but since all the bars closed he has been forced to hone his act in his basement. He works on his jokes, rewording them endlessly; he watches a lot of YouTube videos of other comics and makes notes on their routines, their choice of worlds, their sense of time, their inflection.

He has a massive cork board with index cards pinned to it which have the breakdown of the routines written on them. It resembles a board you would see in a detective's office who is trying to track a serial killer, with different colored strings running between the victims and the locations of their graves, where they were abducted from etc. Only on Jeff's board we see the jokes and the punchlines.

## INT: BASEMENT-DAY

JEFF LYDON, a forty six year old white male, bounds into the frame and waves. He begins doing his stand-up comedy routine

> ### JEFF
> Hey everybody, great to be here!
> Hey, you guys ever order pancakes in a restaurant and they give you that big lop of butter? Man, what's up with that?

Jeff pauses and thinks.

> ### JEFF (MORE TO HIMSELF)
> I mean, what's up with that?
> What up with that? Yo, what up with that? Sup with that?

Jeff is very aware of his movements; he is obviously thinking about them.
Jeff is not satisfied. He picks up a clipboard and makes a note. He then walks towards the camera, out of frame and shuts it off.

Jeff records and rerecords his act, which he watches over and over. He pours over every detail, every nuance: his hand gestures, the way he raises an eyebrow, his pauses, his posture. He analyzes his act relentlessly.

Jeff's plan, and you have to admire this, is to perform his act on Facebook Live. It is hardly the ideal platform for stand-up comedy but Jeff is determined; he is absorbing the obstacle.

## INT: BASEMENT-NIGHT

### JEFF
**What's the deal with all that butter?**

The thing is, there is no deal with all that butter. But Jeff doesn't understand that.

Why?

He is not funny.

## INT. KITCHEN-DAY

**PAMELA LYDON, a forty-three-year-old white female, sits at the kitchen table with her laptop open and her phone next to it. She is wearing a nurse's uniform. She is looking at the unemployment site for Massachusetts and talking with her sister, KAREN JONES, a forty-year-old white woman, via FaceTime on her phone.**

### PAM
**So, he doesn't qualify for unemployment**

because he quit his job in February.

KAREN

Great timing on that.

PAM

I know but who knew this was going to happen?

KAREN

Did you get your stimulus check?

PAM

I got mine but he didn't get his yet.

KAREN

Well, it's a good thing you're working.

PAM

Yeah, great.

TREVOR (0S)

Mommy, the computer froze again.

PAM

I gotta go. Trevor's doing his remote learning.


Pamela Lydon, Jeff's wife, works as a nurse and is not at all happy to be the sole earner in the home while her husband is in the basement telling jokes. He can't even get unemployment because he quit his job as opposed to being laid off. She is on the verge of divorcing him. She talks to her sister, Karen, via Skype about their situation.

INT. HOME OFFICE-DAY

TREVOR LYDON, an eight-year-old white male,

appears on the screen for his online class.

He is holding up a picture that he has drawn of his

family.

> TREVOR
>
> My mom is a nurse and she works
>
> at the hospital taking care of sick people.
>
> She is a hero because she is making sick
>
> people feel better and they need her right now.

We hear the voice of his teacher, MS. MURIEL.

> MS. MURIEL
>
> Oh, isn't that wonderful! Your mommy
>
> is a hero! And is that your daddy?

> TREVOR
>
> Yes.

> MS. MURIEL
>
> And what does he do?

> TREVOR
>
> He quit his job to tell jokes in the basement.

Their eight year old son, Trevor, is doing his online learning using Google Classroom, which is not going great which is something else that is stressing Pam out. Like many little kids, he gives his teacher and classmates a little window into the situation at home.

**INT. EXTERIOR HOUSE-DAY**

**ANGIE LYDON, an eighteen year old white female, sits on the steps talking on FaceTime to SARAH WHEATON, an eighteen year old female of color.**

> **ANGIE**
> **I know, I really do not want to be living at home my first year of college. I was supposed to be in Florida in August and now it's fucking UMass.**

> **SARAH**
> **I know. I was supposed to be in Arizona.**

> **ANGIE**
> **God, I gotta get out of this house.**

> **SARAH**
> **What day is this?**

Pam and Jeff's daughter, Angie, is disappointed that since the dorms are closed, she cannot go to FSU to play lacrosse and now must attend UMass Amherst and live at home.

The script was written in context of the Coronavirus; we see the effects throughout the film. If I couldn't work around the lockdown, why not just embrace it and use it in the film. Have the characters doing what we are all doing right now: using Zoom, Google Classroom and FaceTime. They wear masks and use hand sanitizer relentlessly. They are staying six feet apart.

They are feeling isolated and frustrated.

So, the Coronavirus morphed from being a problem to become an opportunity. I really never would have thought of using Zoom, Facebook Live, and Google Classroom as plot devices; it would really not have made much sense at any other time and ten years ago they didn't even exist. But not only do they work for the story, they make it a lot easier to shoot and keep everyone safe; most of the actors don't need to be on set; they will be at home in front of their computers on an actual Zoom call or Google Meet. Without this technology the project would not be possible.

**INT. BASEMENT-DAY**

**Jeff is having a Zoom conference with members of his comedy workshop.**

**One of the men, LYLE WHITTLE, a white man in his twenties, is dressed as a Mime and doing an act with a ventriloquist doll that is the same make-up.**

Lyle finishes his routine and addresses the group.

                    LYLE
            So, I was trying to cross genres.

There is a pause as the other members contemplate
this.
FRANK LITTLETON, a white man in his mid-forties,
speaks first.

                    FRANK
            Yeah, I can see that.


JESSICA SMITH speaks.

                    JESSICA
            Yeah, lot to work with there.
Lot to develop.

                    JEFF
            Did you guys watch my video?

                    FRANK
            Yeah, your delivery is really improving.

                    JEFF
            What about the "lop of butter" routine?
MICHAEL PARKER chimes in.

                    MICHAEL
            It's got potential, definitely.

JESSICA

I don't know what a "lop" is. I always

thought that was a verb. Like you "lop off"

someone's head.

JEFF

It's a big hunk of butter. I'm using "lop"

because I can really hit the "p" sound.

MICHAEL

It's so hard to get the timing of a routine

down with no crowd, there's no laughs

or applause.

LYLE

I know. I need an open mic or something.

JEFF

Well, I'm doing the Facebook Live

on June 23rd. You guys are gonna tune in?


They all agree that they will.

FRANK

Okay, guys, we are under a minute here

so next week, same time, same place.

Work on your material and spread the

word about Jeff's performance on the 23rd.


They agree and sign off.

Comedians are a strange lot. There is always a measure of desperation, like this is the last chance at validation. What compels people to get up in front of a group of strangers and try to make them laugh? What are they looking for?

These are the concepts, the philosophy. But the rubber has to meet the road. We need to be able to get these ideas on film.

- Casting

Other than writing the script, casting is the most essential part of the process of getting ready to make a film. You can have the greatest script in the world but it will be ruined by a bad actor or someone who is just not right for the part. Normally what happens is actors send in headshots for the various roles. For many roles, the director is looking for a certain type. He or she can look through head shots and see who does not fit the type and put them aside. (It is amazing how many ignore the casting instructions and send in their material anyway. For example, the role might call for a Caucasian woman in her mid-twenties and you get a headshot of a Hispanic woman in her forties. I guess they feel like they might as well take a shot.)

After having put aside the definite "no's" we would contact actors to come in for an audition. They come on a certain day to an audition space and read for a role. Even though the director has a certain type in mind for certain roles but it is important to keep an open mind. A person might surprise you and do a reading that makes you rethink the character. We put out ads on casting sites and for the three principal roles: Jeff, Angie, and Pam. He then compiled their headshots, resumes and videos into a spreadsheet and sent them to me. I watched the videos and made a list of whom should be called back.

Because of the pandemic, we would be using Zoom for the call backs. This did not make me feel comfortable. I had some serious reservations about only seeing actors on a small screen and not meeting them in person. It somehow didn't feel right to not be in the same room with them to get a sense of their physicality. For one character in particular, I needed to know how tall the actors auditioning for that role were and there really is no way to tell that from Zoom. It felt unnatural but there really wasn't any way around it. If we had demanded that the actors had to come in person then I am sure many of them would have declined.

- Wardrobe

What are the actors going to wear? This is an essential consideration. The clothing needs to reflect the character. I envision that Jeff would wear the standard white shirt, tie and blazer. Something that is rather confining.

- Scheduling

When shooting a film, time is literally money. The schedule needs to be airtight. The more time spent on set, the more it costs. The reason that many people run out of money is due to poor planning. They waste time trying to figure out what they are going to shoot and don't finish (make the day, in film parlance). What scenes are going to be shot on day one, day two, day three? How many days are going to be needed to get this done?

The more time you waste, the more money you waste.

- Shot Lists

What shots are needed to complete each scene. You and the Director of Photography need to sit down and make a list of the shots that are needed. You need to be realistic about what you can get. What seems simple on paper can often become very difficult and time consuming. Work this out ahead of time.

- Props

Make a list of the props that are needed for each scene. Someone needs to be put in charge of making sure that all of these props are on set when they are needed.

- Art Design

When working on a small budget, it is necessary to prioritize. What is the one thing that you really want to design well? What do you really want the audience to see that will resonate with the theme of the production?

These are the somewhat mundane tasks that need to be addressed to make a quality film. But there is value in each one. It's always a balance between the big picture and the details.

**INT: VAN-DAYNIGHT**
**The delivery man drives the streets. We see the effects of the Coronavirus: people wearing masks, restaurants with tables outside, signs thanking workers, Black Lives Matter Signs, Back the Blue signs, Trump/Pence signs, Biden/Harris signs.**
**As he drives he listens to a podcast about the pandemic and the presidential campaign and the protests.**

The Coronavirus looms over everything we do these days. We can feel it. We can't see it or hear it or smell it, but we know it is there, all around us, every day, affecting everything we do. And so the Coronavirus needs to be a character in the film. I needed something or someone to bring a sense of an impending event, something scary and unknown; the audience feels it coming but doesn't know what it is. It is a nameless, relentless force that is moving towards its final destination.

A delivery man. He will be the Coronavirus. Even without the pandemic people were getting everything delivered, even more so these days because they are scared to go to the stores.

The delivery man driving through the streets gives a sense of motion and momentum to the story; something is happening, something is about to happen.

Pending, something is pending. Like a vaccine or another lockdown or another spike in cases, something is always on the horizon, around the corner.

But what is he delivering? To whom? Is it salvation or doom? Or both?


I love these characters; I truly do. Especially Jeff. He will do whatever it takes to complete his routine and get it out there in front of people. As misguided as it is, he believes in himself.

I want to believe in myself. I have never had a short film accepted into a film festival.. The last one I did was rejected from the twenty three festivals that we entered. Making a short film may be misguided; maybe I don't have the talent to do it well. Maybe other people see my work and say, "God, that is so bland. So lame."

Maybe I should just be realistic and stop dumping thousands of dollars into short films that go nowhere.

But I'd rather be misguided.

# Break of Day

By Anannya Dasgupta

# Insidious

By Ruchira Mandal

Winter
Sunshine
Trickles
Past curtains—
Insidious
Longings
Disguised
As warmth.
Our
Unspoken
Dreams
Unmask
Who
We
Are.

# A Night on the Town, and Life Isn't Fair

By Shannon Frost Greenstein

"You're doin' it wrong, bro."

The man is Black,
homeless,
struggling,
a veteran,
forgotten.
Because life isn't fair.

We are dressed to the nines
Center City Philadelphia
an evening of ostentatious luxury awaiting.

"You should be walking on her other side."

He corrects my husband mildly
a helpful tidbit
a vestige of Emily Post.
And I wonder;

Where did he learn this rule of etiquette?
Was it as a boy, on his mother's lap,
Because, of course, every homeless person has a mother,
is someone's son or daughter
but life isn't fair.

And as we smile at him
and acknowledge my husband's faux pas,
my eyes well with all the potential
in front of me
if drugs and mental illness and systemic racism and inequality

did not warp the playing field.

My husband switches to walk on my other side.

"Now you got it."

And I see the man.
See him.
See him as a human.
And life isn't fair
and life is confusing
and life is uncontrollable.

But at least archaic rules can show us the way
as my husband guards me from the street
in my silk gown.

We pass the man
who has no bed
in which to sleep tonight
but knows how to treat a lady.
And life isn't fair.

# Untitled

By Ann Privateer

# By the Nape

By William Barker

The world is quiet
at this earliest of hours.

My cat lounges atop
the desk pushing a pen around

until it falls to the ground.
Having no concept of time,

she is awake only because I am.
Difficult to fathom an existence

of such profundity and freedom,
but for the length of a poem,

an indulgent duration
where I see the universe

through a detailed lens,
like a horologist

hunched over
an antique watch.

# A Receptacle of Shock

By Dr. Emily Bilman

Hortansia stepped on the train that was on time and on track. She was a multi-lingual translator for a pharmaceutical company. She disliked the special effort she had to make not to trespass the frame of the allocated seat. All the rituals Hortansia constantly performed to lose weight, her strict dieting, the constant control of her weight, accompanied by exercises in the week-ends, had reduced her waist line and a few centimeters off her thighs. Obsessively, she measured her body once a week. Oh! How she envied the lean dainty figure of the young woman sitting next to her.

She rebelled against her efforts which drained all her energy and reached out for the chocolate cookie neatly wrapped up in transparent cellophane paper in her bag. It was a chocolate cookie with three varieties of chocolate she had baked with great attention. The cookie's contours were shaped irregularly by the cooking yet, it still maintained its supple onctuosity. As she teethed the cookie, she felt each grain of flour, each grain of sugar melt on her palate. Like an opiate, she felt the sugar infuse and satiate her brain. She felt well. She loved the reward of a chocolate cookie even more when she was asked to finish the extra sheets of accounting on the week-ends at home. She could hardly say "No" to anyone.

In fact, her refuge in food was a vicious circle. When she was frustrated, she had to eat a sweet bar or a chocolate cookie but; then, she had to compensate for the unconscious guilt of yielding to temptation by eating yet another one. Deep down inside she know that she would always seek comfort food to soothe her anxiety; yet, food would also widen her emptiness like a never-ending well. She would keep on consuming the sweet rewards she failed to attain in real life.

She thought of her mother's depression. Her mother could not bear her father's increasing inner and physical violence when the civil war broke out in her country the 90's. Her father was a sturdy man with tanned skin and piercing olive-green eyes. He was the middle child of an extensive family of six brothers. He had peasant origins and linked with strong ties to his native land.

When fighting began, he brought out his guns, oiled them, and began shooting on the trees outside the barn. He had sworn to fight the enemy until his last drop of blood. As the family slowly disintegrated, he began to drink heavily. He drank and drank some more. The more violent he became, the more her mother sank into depression until deep apathy silenced her like the heavy mist covering the near-by mountains on autumn evenings.

Hortansia, then fifteen, decided to run away from home leaving her family behind. She left her home with the little money that she had earned as a baby-sitter, traversed fields and forests, and walked all the way to the check-point. Then, she reached her relative's home in the capital where she obtained her refugee pass to Switzerland within the span of a week. She still recollected her mother's broken voice when she announced it to her on the phone.

Like the trail rails that separate into branches to reach different cities, she, of course, realized that her father's addiction to alcohol and his aggression which triggered her mother's depression were the unconscious causes of her obesity. Her parents' addictions and anxieties were passed on to her as an inter-generational unease that her body had to contain. So she succumbed to a vicious circle of binge eating as a substitute. These were the many factors that almost influenced her epigenetically.

Yet, in her integrative writing courses which combined sessions of psychotherapy with expressive autobiographical writing, Hortansia realized that her mother's depression had even deeper roots. In fact, her mother was the victim of hunger and deprivation even before her marriage. Her mother's state of deprivation was also due to material dispossession during the independence war. The nexus of epigenetics was aggrandized and transmitted to Hortansia's body which absorbed the physical and affective shocks of her mother's generation.

When she arrived in Geneva, she was turned down from many jobs and received myriad rejection letters that depressed her to the point of accepting her fate as if it were normal. The frustration of not finding a proper job which would assure her independence added to her anxiety. Hortansia  had felt depressed like  a dried-out flower depleted of oxygen in a stifling atmosphere. No job, no boyfriend, no social relations. And so many tribulations.

The train reached Thurville. Hortansia  looked plaintively at the gentleman standing by train door and asked for help to descend the two steps leading to the platform. He extended his hand to her. She appreciated his gesture but also felt aggressive towards him because she, unconsciously, hated being dependent on anyone. The bitter memory of the fratricidal war and the consequent disintegration of her family were the motives behind her cleavage she had so meticulously written about in her integrative therapy.

She crossed the underground passage that led to her office. On her way picked up a newspaper with a large heading "Obese people are at a higher risk of morbidity during the Covid-19 pandemic". That was the last stroke! Masked and gloved, she reached her office on the sixth floor. Her colleague, Martha, greeted her. Hortansia:

-   " I read today that Covid-19 virus sheds its RNA when it enters the organs and produces its own lipids and also enables the lipids of the other cells to replicate. I also discovered in my integrative writing classes that deprivation and constant relapse factors due to guilt are the unconscious causes of obesity which resembles heroin addiction aggravated by the lack of methadone."

-   Martha: "You should not worry about Covid and drug addiction now. You need to take care of your body before your bariatric surgery. If you eat lots of fruits and vegetables, walk or swim daily, and continue going to the gym and your integrative classes your surgery will succeed."

- "I guess you are right but confinement and social distancing augment the risk factors, too; for we feel isolated and vulnerable but hate ourselves for doing so."

- "Did you see the translation that was left on your desk this morning? It's about a new treatment for obesity based on enzymes called leptin-peptides that act as ghelin-suppressors that regulate food-reward by the amygdala. The effect is gradual weight loss."

- "I will contact the company and ask for a trial sample."

Hortansia progressed with her translation that dealt with the intricate relation of the amygdala or our primitive instinctive brain with our reward system. The gastrointestinal peptides regulated weight loss so that the body no longer needed a reward system as an intake of food or even drugs.

Then, she called up Pepsom S.A. She explained her condition and asked to try the new treatment as a palliative for her obesity. The Director's secretary, Mrs. Müller, answered the phone:

- "We cannot issue a trial sample because we sold the license of the peptides. The peptide treatment cannot be obtained in Switzerland because the trials are not yet conclusive here. Once they become conclusive and all the side-effects known, the peptide treatment can then, be commercialized."

- "More than 650 million people suffer from obesity in the world. We all know that it is a chronic disease that escalates in jolts of several kilos a year. I cannot understand how this treatment which is valid for another country cannot be used here where more than 15% of the population suffers from obesity. Is your marketing department working on this crucial matter?"

- "Since the trials are not yet finalized, we cannot commercialize the treatment."

- "It seems strange that the only concrete choice left for the obese in this country is bariatric surgery when a palliative treatment based on peptides exists which would prevent the cost of the operation that also removes significant gut peptides and enzymes from the intestines. Our guts are our second brain, after all."

Confronted to a definitive refusal from Mrs. Müller, Hortansia did not want to continue the conversation. She was unable to convince her. Research showed that the reward system of the obese is deregulated so that after prolonged periods of weight control, obese bodies even respond to rewards negatively. Hortansia felt weak and began to shiver as if taken by fever. When her requests were negated, her body somatized her frustrations by feeling cold tremors to absorb the shock-effect.

At half past six, Hortansia was back on the train that would take her to her integrative writing class. That evening they were writing about the body-image. Hortansia wrote about apples, pears, quinces, mangoes, pineapples, and bananas to highlight the diversity of body shapes. The participants' smiling faces showed they were impressed. She felt happy.

A week later, Hortansia received a letter from her relatives with her father's new address. It read: "After your father was imprisoned by the guerilla group, he escaped to the checkpoint and left the country. In the free zone, he joined a human rights organization active in fighting ethnic cleansing which operates in schools, charities, syndicates, and NGO's. I'm sending you the address. Stay safe."

Hortansia knew that she inherited her steel-will from her father's will to survive. She would visit and tell him that and more. She would finally abandon the girdled weight of the world around her waistline like a bomb ready to explode.

# A Conversation Between The Day and I
By Steven Rossi

Today is not any day, today is *the* day
no different than any other and despite being the same
I will make you special promises because I decided
it was time to start acting on life instead of watching it
so whether they are for you or the part of me you see, it won't
matter
and don't get me started because
it is too early for prose and metaphors, after all
the day is simple and after a lot of thinking
I concluded I too am simple, quite
so once you wake me from my simple dream on my simple pillow
I got from a retail store I can no longer remember the name of
but wish I did because sometimes I get strangely attached to things
like my idea of trying something new today

you'll play along as you tend to
for reasons you hold close and when I ask why you say
you can decide for yourself, why does it matter?
but that isn't the point

we agree to sip coffee on the balcony after we shower off yesterday
we joke about how I almost clogged the drain with yesterday's I
have not washed off
for years

and you laugh and tell me something like

It's about time!

l chuckle slightly embarrassed but persistent nevertheless and say

I am a new man! I promise

among other promises like to love and nurture you

build you up brick by brick and

give to you until nothing is left


then you remind me that despite my every intention to change

I have always been the person you have loved and nurtured

made a home out of when you laid the foundation with the utmost

care

and have given to when I had nothing to offer in return


I realize this too is simple and I have once again overthought

what else is new?

# Crisis

By Tali Cohen Shabtai

It was an

in ten sive

acquaintance

I did not know

that the mind is illusive

and paracetamol is not admissible

for a psychosomatic sense

in the pelvis.

That the thought sticks

like a Band-Aid on a congealed wound

in the morning

and secretes pus until tomorrow,

and at night an emotional baggage

uncompromisingly hard

and impossible to reject.

I did not know

that "bias for my own good" according to

the attribution theory

did validate an "inverted bias"

between action and between the interior and the exterior

at a time of depression.

After all, I am from there

where a man hosts himself first

and places in deposit

the absence of neurotransmitters

in his nervous system

-to-

a two-month encounter on blue

chairs in the unit's lobby.

Surely I am where

Dahlia Ravikovitch* was for "a ship

without sails in a sea without wind"


But I still

admire human smiles

in the most undeclared way

there is

I am in crisis.


*An Israeli poet.

## "Absolutely"

By Jeanette Willert

...the host concurs while interviewing
his pod-cast guest.  *"Absolutely"* that is what
the poet meant in that line.  The two murmur
and concur once more to seal the deal
on that particular poetic line. Its fate,
*raison d'être*, now etched in blunt, cemetery font.

*"Absolutely!",*
a common response,
the speaker in a hurry
to form alliance, to still the pool
of possible discord or discovery.

I have begun to hunger for a tentative "...maybe"
or (more daring) "if you really think about it...".
Talking together has become a ride
dependent on both people hoisting their weight
into an agreed-upon cadence, a seesaw.

At least on a carousel you can dismount
the bobbing horse and change steeds or
head for the fun-house or a game arcade
to shoot, at will, for a furry prize you choose.

# Listener

By Karol Nielsen

Over dinner, she told us her ideas about the news and politics while we listened. She had been in my writer's group and we remained close even though the group no longer met. She stopped herself and said, I'm doing all the talking; neither of you has said a word. Her friend chimed in with a little something but her soft spoken voice was hard to hear in the noisy French bistro. We briefly discussed my essay that had been published in a literary magazine but I couldn't sustain the momentum. She went went back to talking about the news and politics and we were quiet. When I told my mother what happened, she said she stopped being embarrassed by her silence when she realized a family friend she respected was silent, too. The world needs listeners, she said, and I listened to her.

# Directions When The Path Ahead Berates You

By Steven Rossi

1. Speak with soft hands and spells,
unravel your fists and watch the fingers freefall
tell them of magic and watch them
line forgiveness on the numb of your ear.

2. Leave your skin tucked into last night's new moon. Rip up the
bills and all your big plans and the to do's and reorder the scraps
into new beginnings until you recognize the words looking back at
you.

3. Fill the tank until it's overflowing like dawn over yesterday, then
slam the gas until the road starts to sing operas of blazed rubber.

4. Be weary of the doubt rooted in your ravines. Head up as high
as you can go. Scale a mountain or three until the earth bleeds into
the sky while you listen to the altitude teach you to speak anew.

5. Say a little prayer to remember all you've passed by.

Though forgetting and leaving grow in the same garden, they do
not nourish us the same. When harvesting, one leaves us endlessly
hungry, while the other prepares the soil for the seasons to come.

6. To truly quench your thirst, drink from the lake where life
converges. Nourish yourself in the paradise of now as innocently as
the foxes and deer. Scoop from your reflection a drop at a time
until you remember it's nothing more than a life in passing as
fragile as a tide.

And as you watch the water looking back at you
ask yourself, "Did I ever leave?"

# Polaroid

By Jenn Powers

# Lighting Shadowed Designs
By Bill Cushing

While singularly high on chem-trail theories,

a mad Ulysses whose image might hide past

icons for a lucid siren whose image

might hide past icons. Then he saw himself

in others, survived by living more obscure

and even stranger lives. Elements of surprise

invited a state of being, frighteningly

similar and rivaling unself-conscious

recycling, twisting reality slightly

when the muse struck hard and fast and repeatedly

with a club. Images, like party crashers,

with faces that clash with nature, fractured color,

shade, or hue. Lives are altered forever

through brute evolution of thought, and living, like

finding Nessie—ever sought yet rarely seen,

dissolves into a series of hallucinations.

# The Theory of Survival

By Ololade Akinlabi Ige

tell me, how do i paint myself in this poem?
there are faces that overshadow the mirror.
i mean somewhere, a boy scours for a home in his wound.
this poem is a chariot trailing back its broken verses.

i dashed out of my father's house on a cold December
and walked through winding paths where men were saturated into
silence. in the feast of grief everyone mourns their lost days.
at the wrist of a road a man sings Nina's
and my mother resurrected in my body.

i do not find a home for my past till it became
a broken river in my body. i carried my dreams
on my slouching shoulders & hunted for home
in drowning cities. a body sings for itself a lullaby
in the absence of heed.

this poem is a chariot trailing back its broken verses.
if halfway a poem died, would it find a tomb in an omnibus?
a bird lost it way home and built for itself a new nest. mind you,
hope is like a sky.

# The Bard of Frogtown

By A Whittenberg

Like most writers I am full of shit.

Sometimes I look at the piles and piles of half started prose and think, "Got a match?"

And then, I think, I'll write a poem. Poems save paper.

So all of a sudden I am a poet. Yet, I still have nothing to say.

Write, writer, write! Goddamn it, write you fucking idiot. Asshole, hole in the ass. Craphead. Son of a bitch!

Hey!

What?

Don't get personal.

By the way, my real father, yes, the one I have never seen in my life, is a goddamn poet. My mother still gets an occasional sestina through the mail from his as yet to be published chapbook entitled, The Part of Me that No One Knows.

Tell me about it.

Yet as a poet, I just don't feel like I am any good. When I was younger I used to read my stuff with a sense of accomplishment. Now I just cringe. After work I come home and try to get busy on something gold and it turns on trite, banal, and unkempt.

Children are natural artists then they get old and they dry up. I am 19 now. And as I keep saying I have nothing to say.

I've lived with Debra for the past four years.

When I left home it was like a funeral except no one had died. I was so sad. I cried once I hit the main drag. Big tears, buckets of them.

I was fifteen, when Debra and I found our own place. We moved from a little town to a big city. From West to East while still staying North. We live in rough and tumble Frogtown. In Frogtown, us people sell crafts, they line the drags with their handufactured baskets, pottery, metal works, and textiles.

She is a little bit older than me and helped me out a great deal. Not just with the security deposit but she listen to me hash out about my childhood. Long nights we spent therapeutically bottle and blunt passing till I got it all out, the words. I realized now that not only do I hate my stepfather, but I also resent my younger brother, and that my mother is a continual source of frustration.

With all that memesized and catharsis size, I should crack open like an egg. I should have plenty to write about. I should look at a blank piece of paper and fill it.

I wash airplanes for a living.

Somebody has to.

I wake up at five in the AM and go down to the airport and scrub the thick plastic windows with a long handled brush. I have always loved planes, always dreamed of

floating above things.  Tempting God with man made angel
wings.

When I got home this afternoon, Debra was in broken-in
jeans, a teal tee shirt and the familiar fawn colored
leather jacket.  She wears all of this indoors because we
have limited heat.  Sometimes the walls get frost-covered
Still, Debra is a diligent writer.  She does songs.  I walk
in an she is holding the guitar pick between her teeth as
She scribbles notes on a page.  She flicks her head back an
winks at me.  She is a winker.  Always winking, an I think
just who in the hell wears the pants in this relationship.

She does.

Debra loves bits of clutter: Books and papers and
hankies that she blew her nose on.  I can't stand it.
Often I just want to tidy up but dare I take liberties with
her, her, her -- well, I suppose genius is as good a word
as any.

But perhaps it's still not the right one.

A few months ago, Debra sold one of her songs to a big
deal Cosmopolitan company.  She got 500 dollars outright.  We had
steak for a week.  That's the problem with being a Zoe and dealing
with the Cosmos everything you sell is sold
outright and haven't us Blacks have given enough away.
They have stolen our land, our women, now our music.

The name of the song was, "A White Sleeve of
Moonlight."  And when Debra sang it felt Black.  It was
textual and lilting yet bodacious as cowboys.  She used

steel strings instead of the Cosmopolitan twinkling of a
piano. I heard the Cosmo version on the radio and I almost
kept passing the dial. It was a totally different song,
and a corny one at that.

Oh Debra... She was the sanctuary from my problems I
forgot she had so many of her own. She was like an regular
Zoe with a family tree that tangled at the root. I could
never get it straight but I knew she was the half sister of
the dead Rice Street Man. The Rice Street Man that my
brother, Jak, was so enamored with. The Rice Street Man
that smelled worse than his dog. And as if that weren't
bad enough, quite a few of Debra's short on dollars, long
in the tooth relatives used to stay over temporarily for
months and months. And poor little Deb was treated like
she was invisible. She was forced into disappearing to
create a room.

She used to have to give up her bedroom and sleep on the
couch. It was then that she learned to play that funky
old guitar that she'd found in a dumpster. At night while
all the live-ins where raising Hell she'd mouth the words,
practice fingering, playing without sound. Just another
blond haired girl, in a country that over flowed with
them.

So unprettied up, you could take her for granted. I
have never seen her in a dress but then again she's never
seen me in one either. I like to use her life in my
writing even more than I like to use my life in my writing.

Writers are the worst type of people God ever put on
this earth. They note the way the dirt falls on a casket
of a dear friend because they know they can use it later.
It is always my writing, my writing, my writing. The whole
fucking world revolves around my writing.

I want to write a poem.

Lovers make the worst critics, so why do I always ask
my Debra?

I show her my words few and she says, "I don't know it
sort of sticks in my throat."

I snatches the paper back from her and tell her that
she was supposed to fucking read it not fucking eat it.

She laughs at me. She laughs at me. She throws her
lovable head back and laughs at me.

I read my work aloud:

Salt without bread.

~~Thorns on a cactus.~~

Buddy Holly, I miss you.

Why didn't you go Greyhound?

I smile, puffing my chest out. Sure, it needs some
revision but its not all bad. The images are clear and
concrete. The sound and rhythm may need some spit and
polish.

All right, it sucks.

It bites the big wiener.

But at least it has punctuation and it does not employ
the lowercase "i".

I want to be Langston Hughes.

Enough of these meditations. These scream fests on the mysteries of freedom, love, and hate.

I want to be remembered.

I know I am not a great writer I am only a great re writer. Half the time there is nothing pithy in the first draft. Half the time I don't know where its going its all improved. I don't have a style or tone that I wish to effect. I feel like screaming at myself where is my theme? Where is my message? Why am writing this poem in the first place.

I will switch back to prose.

Inside every fiction writer there is a failed poet.

Metaphors, like my heart is dry like a big red balloon, are inflated but then I think all right so where where do I go from there?

I break for supper. Debra fixed homemade pizza pie with marmot meat and shrooms as topping. I down a few pizza slices and drop the crust. She's not a bad cook, but I'm a little better, I measure, I do not gestamate so much. She has a great smile, nothing but teeth. Big teeth and squinchy eyes. I enjoy this time a couple of low rent artists eating pizza off a white plate with blue trim. She asks me about the planes and I tell her quite recently they had entrusted me with an unbelievable amount of keys.

"How many is too many to believe?"

"37."

"Unbelievable," she winks at me. "Now don't fly off with the place."

I stand and she makes a grab for my butt, smiling, " Off to do more writing?" she asked.

"That's a good question," I answer.

After our meal she washes the dishes and I take my compositions to the bedroom.

In this next expanse of time, I had done everything to write. I drew a bath, drank some murk, splashed cold water in my ears, danced the bop, the bump, the butterfly, the electric slide, the four corners, the icky shuffle, the mashed potato, the shingling, the worm. I felt refreshed, but still no words.

So I light up and dream, I was make love to Debra only she has thick black hair and the wind blows and exposed her blond roots. Her eyeliner ran down her cheeks like fast graffiti. Those long full breasts had shrunk to teacups.

I dream of white food as symbolism. Rice pudding and glazed doughnuts.

SPACE. Time and space. Time sitting, smoking in the numb silence, watching the snow, as if it were doing something wild, like disappearing instead of the same old same old. I press my face against the pane and gaze at the wide, white city below.

Winter. Heavy snowstorms at the floodgates bringing up a whirlpool of memories. Snowing as marvelous as sugar -- pink and white candy coated Christmas.

Debra, her bland blue eyes told of a fairy tale of
cabbage and rye toast.  Toy soldiers.  Debra vouting a
rendition of "White Christmas".  I start singing along
real low and soft you'd have to read my kisser to tell.
Wilting.

The soundtrack mixes over and over.

"Are you gonna share or is a contact high all that I
can hope for?" is the question that wakes me.

Debra stands by the doorway, 25 years old, and wasting
her time on me.  I'm just an adult child still so full of
dream.  Unable to achieve any synthesis.

I roll a herb her way.

Sometimes it's better not to force it I think as my
ram road is in her and I'm frictioning her.  Sometimes it's
better to distill in the hope of further cross
fertilization.

I do have a beginning of something:
Snow like sweat
or smoke, like mercury,
rising above itself
in a cloud.

# You'll be Snow White

By Linda M. Crate

you want to call me monster
so i polished my claws,
and scrubbed these fangs white as the moon;
woke up my dark feminine so i could
be wholly me
again—

little werewolf,
you can pray to the moon
all you want
she is my mother and she won't save you;

the only one she'll save is me

i hope you're ready to meet death
because soon she'll be your
only lover—

you didn't respect me so now you have
to die

because i have no light or love to spare you
only rage, only wrath, only ruin remain
for you;

so go ahead and take a bite of my old heart
it will be the poisoned apple that kills you—

no princess will be every to wake
you from your eternal slumber,
little prince;

you'll be snow white.

# Ordinary Moments

By Thomas Zampino

Memories came flooding back today.

Simple things, like when I grabbed your

hand for the very first time, and when

you touched my hand for the very last.

Two ordinary moments that forever mixed

up everything, that set everything on fire

before we ever learned about forgetting.

Ordinary moments are sometimes like that.

Even if memories are not.

# Untitled

By Ann Privateer

# A Love that Defies Death

By Madeleine McDonald

Each breath hurt, but the dying woman knew peace, for she remembered a shaman's words from long ago, some time in the travelling years of her youth. Despite the hocus-pocus of smoke and drums, despite the Mongolian guide's odd translation, his message had been unambiguous. "When you die, you go in the light. Someone wait for you, with love that defies death." That message had sustained her during a long widowhood and soon she would see her beloved husband again.

The portal opened. The light beckoned. The dying woman recoiled, her limbs jerking as she fought to release the grip of a guy she had slept with twice at university because she felt sorry for him.

END

# Life As a Cliché

By Allison Whittenberg

So trite, my boss, stereotypically balding, puts his

hands on my shoulder while I was processing words instead

of word processing. Are you some kind of writer? he asks.

When I don't answer, his hands move up to play with my

earrings, which dangle parallel to my cheekbones.

Can you work late tonight? He wants to know.


So, I had to fuck him. Certainly, I can't support

myself off my anemic symbolism, my flabby free verse. I need

to keep my clerical skills employed.


So the next morning, during dictation, in my

embroidered white blouse, crisp to the point of snapping, I

remain unaltered. Our eyes meet: his loaded with metaphor;

mine without the least suggestion of allusion.

# Spellbound

By Linda Imbler

How they must have loved;
before the roses turned
into prisons and tragedies.
Each of their ghosts will later quarrel,
accusing the others of loving only themselves.
Weeping together as they fall
from the watchtower of jubilation,
where beautiful birds roosted and sung.
They prayed for passion to be
brought back from that first time.
Prayers for a wonderful straying,
back to that long-belated return,
that sometime describe as peace on Earth.

They dug,
into secret mines of strange melancholy,
in the hopes of rediscovering
the enchantment of love,
love being that other spell
that twins with foresight.
They bore,
the weight of mostly sorrow
while their future was unforeseen,
until they realized that having dreams,
even ones not yet come true,
can guide them toward that happy future.

# Notice the Scent of Blood Between My Lines

By Perla Kantarjian

*To Beirut*


i slither upon you

in the afternoons

of Sundays when the men are in their homes

by their wives their mothers

sleeping away the heaviness of their

fleshy fleshy meals

instead of squirting

their eyes and tongues outwards.


on Sunday afternoons it is calm

almost,

and I slither upon your

calling grounds-

your streets become my riverbed

and I become your river

flowing flowing in quasi-comfort,

never yet whole.


remember, I am a woman, and upon your streets

women are yet unwelcome

to walk alone

there are

creaky cracks in your fractured infrastructure

and *women are vulnerable*

everywhere *everywhere is unsafe*

your father brother uncle husband citizens warn

(but only to your women.)


you and I have both been broken open

and contaminated.

your undying wars left you marred with ruptures

incessant

oozing blood

in place of Tyrian Purple.

yet i look at you

breathing

through the crevices

daringly-

you inspire me

and all your women.


remember, you and us have been both broken open

and intimidated.

yet we do not mind to die bleeding while

we stitch ourselves

into form

for we know what happens

when we remain threadbare

static

open.


remember, they called your October revolution female

and the headlines wondered what it is

that pulling force that bound us

your women

to the frontline

of the uprising for months

for months! they roared-

little did they know

we have been on the frontline

fighting

for years

and years.


we yet remain

unanswered

but never at a standstill-

never without a needle and a thread

in our bruised palms

tying our own goddamn seams.

# A Suadela's Shardoma
By Bill Cushing

I feel the
edge of her nails as
her hand strokes
my arm. Her
inked dragonfly succumbs to
the art of longing,

painting life
when, from the corner
of the bed,
one bare and
bended leg beckons, and I
lightly kiss her thigh.

# In Solitude

By Chahat Soneja

# Street Madonna

By Catherine Alexander

(Published in Rosebud, Issue 29, April 2004 And The
Anthology Project, University of Washington, Vol. 2, Issue 1,
June 2007)

At the Campo de' Fiori, filled with produce, flowers
and restaurants, a Romani with Spanish eyes, darker than the
shadow she creates, swirls her long, crimson skirt, the pleats
stroking her hips. Small, shapely, advancing hips.

She nudges between converging tables, in search of
the outstretched hand filled with coins, which she finds and
accepts with a nod. Tossing a mane of matted curls, she
adjusts the scarf cradling her child and approaches the next
table where beer-chugging men wrangle over soccer scores.
The Romani stares with insistence, standing feet apart and
hands on hips, her charcoal eyes darting from one man to the
other. Carousers finally look up, sneer and pretend to spit.
She sneers in return, picks up her skirt and clicks her high
heels, which should, but don't, catch in the cobblestones.

If she were a Renaissance painting, she'd be a
Caravaggio—spontaneous, grimy and real. If she were a
marble Bernini with Apollo pressed against her, she'd be no
Daphne.

The truth is she has only the clothes she comes with
and two brassieres, one black and one white.

\* \* \*

A line of priests crosses the Campo. Brother Stefano,
a new priest, steps away to examine the local produce.

Suddenly the Romani appears before him, knotted curls trailing down her back and a scarf of poppies nestling the child at her breast. Her ancient stare suggests a sorcerer, a soothsayer, a witch. But gradually her eyes turn to translucent green, her look as beneficent as the Madonna. Still, she demands a coin for her child. Stefano throws three coins on the cobblestones. As she bends to scoop up the change, the child slips from its scarf hammock. Tiny feet skim the cobblestones, but tiny lips never lose their latch on life. Stefano glares for a second, then rushes from the square.

*　*　*

With laughing *putto* in tow, Madonna quits the Campo de'Fiori, crosses Vittorio Emanuele and heads up the Corso to the Piazza Navona market. In the middle of the boat-shaped square, water spills from Bernini's Fountain of the Four Rivers—the Nile, the Ganges, the Danube and the Rio de la Plata. Madonna worries little about world rivers, Bernini or the Baroque, knows not an obelisk from a column, Domitian from Augustus. Instead, she pays tribute to the street traders and performers—the salesman with a dozen fake Gucci handbags on each arm, two accordion players, a base violinist, and on either side of the fountain, one man painted green and one silver.

As luck would have it, a tour group with orange baseball caps advances in her direction. She ambles up slowly, quickens her step and sashays between the tourists with her palm extended. She tosses her hair, her skirt, clicks her heels. Each time her palm is filled, she slips the coins into her pocket and holds out for more. Finally, the leader with an orange flag shakes it at her, as if she's more odious than the man who has sprayed himself green.

As she ventures on, her breasts begin to swell and she steps into the Pantheon's colonnaded porch to feed her bambino. Then up through the Spanish Steps to the Pincio gardens where she takes her siesta behind a shady palm. When she wakes, a peddler stands before her with two long-stemmed roses, *a buon mercato*. She nods *sì,* clip-clops down the Spanish Steps and marches to S. Ivo alla Sapienza. The chapel is empty except for a coffin waiting for mourners. She sets the roses on the casket, lights a candle and takes a pin from her hair to pick the offering lock. In the Palazzo, she shares her hoist with Romanies hiding in the double arcades, keeping only what she needs.

\* \* \*

At the Vatican, she pockets a few coins before she's caught bare breasted, nursing her Christ child. The *Guarda robba* demolish her just as Bramanté once did the Basilica. She leaves St. Peter's foot unkissed and spurns this holy Grand Central Station. Besides, she's at home on the cobblestones of the Campo de'Fiori. The fish heads in the piazza, the overripe figs and twisted carrots make perfect sense, along with brimmed hats and cheap straw bags.

Madonna knows she won't burn here like Giordano Bruno, poor mad heretic, whose gigantic statue she leans against to count her morning bounty. She's fared well, but nothing like the peddler of jumping Disney mouses and 3-D winking Jesuses on the streets of St. Peters.

\* \* \*

When Madonna was barely 16, a tall man with graying hair and a brooding nature took her to the Isle of Capri. There, flat-roofed homes pressed into jagged rocks that pushed out from the ocean to the top of Anacapri. So unlike Rome, with its grottos, misty air and small, gaudy shops.

The man called himself Emilio and dubbed her Constanza di Roma. He plied her with lilies and seashells, a coral cross and a skirt with three flounces. Next, he sandaled her feet with straps of pearls and anointed her skin with island-made perfumes.

But then he changed. He made her work the grotto while he waited under the bougainvillea and oleander. Afterwards he snatched her purse and abandoned her on the island. The love in Constanza's heart turned as hard as the obsidian beads she stole from the small, gaudy shops.

Madonna ran to the Funicular Railway that jerked down the rocks to the shore. She stowed away on a boat and ended up in Salerno. The clean provincial people and gulf air made her homesick for the Tiber, with its river rats floating on orphaned shoes. Rome's twisted pagan streets and crumbling churches were her history. Campo nights of beer bashing, days under the Titan sun, the perfume of decaying fish and apricots, led her to rapture. Rome, that pure old whore—Madonna was one with her, in this life and the next.

# Sculpture
By CJP Lee

# Body Heat

by Rp Verlaine

The scar of
flawless memories
with stalled replacements
unmarked by doubt
and similarly perfect.


love had escaped us
as if it were a convict
running between searchlights
into a new darkness
promising uncertainty.


Till that summer
running from the train
and the job we shared
zero degrees always
I remember
if I'd blink
the snowflakes on her tongue
would vanish while she looked
for keys to our always
frigid apartment.


We'd abscond indoors
To hide under blankets
Like reprobate arsonists
Fleeing the chill with terror

Till our bodies took hold
Of each other.
Detached yet physical
To elemental truths.
We were lightning in the dark
Each accidental touch
A flashing shower of spark
while exhausting each other
Covered in sweat.


Then winter ended
As did we
I've yet to find
Such a spark
Yes, a flame
In the same bedroom
burning red to blue to white
for her still.

# My Favourite Flower
By Yeshi Choden

Its softness is red and white

and blue and the rest

of a certain shape and a certain size

its beauty grows tall, it sits clustered

it climbs and it sways

I like it infused with the earth

I like it in a vase, no longer of Nature

but still carrying life and wonder

I like it flattened inside a book

dry and strong and then fixed on a card

if I send it

it is my favourite flower I am sending

# The Old Maple

By Swarnav Misra

Contemplating the old maple

So proud Thonet  must have been

Never have I ever seen such bosting burnish

Even the longest sliver,

Is so shy of protruding out

Her legs, majestic foundation

Bearing the belfie of all bulk

Surviving the seasons beyond sufferance

Now the feet have been daubed with dirt

Perhaps, all she needs, is a bath

But all I have is hot briny

But aren't you an old maple?

You are the perfection of erstwhile time,

The Beauty of the bygones,

Celebration of the condemned

While now, obsolete you have become

So my dear Cathedra,

Withstand my burden one last time,

As the Hangman's knot takes care of my lot.

# Untitled

By Bransha Gautier

# White Room

By Elena Brooke

It is a white room. It is a white room with white walls.

I stand in front of a painting. It is a painting of peach and sunset swirls.

The man approaches me in the white room, he is a man in his 60's who has his white hair in a long ponytail. His suit looks pristine.

He speaks to me. "How are you doing this fine day, young lady?"


...I have woken up. I heard a sound nearby. I sat up in bed and stretched my arms. Friday. Today is Friday. As I yawned, I remembered that Tasha had told us some news last night. I could ask her about it over breakfast. I changed into my work clothes on and went downstairs to the kitchen.

Cassie was already up and making a cup of tea, and she offered to make me one as well. I nodded, not trusting my voice just yet.

"...toast," I eventually croaked out.

Cassie gave me a confused look. I coughed to clear my throat.

"I meant to say that I'm making some toast, do you want some as well?"

"I had some already," Cassie replied, "but thanks for asking."

I coughed again with my mouth closed as I grabbed the bread from the bread bin. I placed the bread in the toaster, and went to grab a plate from the cupboard. I noticed Cassie open the fridge and grab the margarine, putting it on the counter for me to use. The only sounds in the kitchen were the kettle boiling and the quiet buzz of the toaster heating up.

I thought back to my sleep last night, and only the image of a white room came to mind. I remembered it being a particularly bright white light, almost blinding. The light in the kitchen looked dim in comparison to the room. The kettle stopped boiling and I heard Cassie pour the hot water into two mugs.

"It's two sugars, right? And milk?" she asked me.

I looked at her, surprised that she remembered. "Yes, that's correct."

"Just like my brother," Cassie replied, giving a small laugh. "Do you have any—"

The interruption had arrived in the form of Tasha screaming from upstairs. Cassie and I looked up at the same time just as the sound of footsteps going downstairs was heard. Tasha ran into the kitchen. She was wearing a turquoise dressing gown and her dirty blonde hair was messy. Tasha was grinning wildly.

"Guys, I got accepted into the competition! Can you believe it? I got in! I just got the email right this second."

"Geez, Tasha. I thought there was a spider in your room or something," Cassie said once Tasha had stopped jumping and talking at us.

Tasha had the sense to look sheepish. "Sorry, I guess I got carried away a bit."

"Congratulations," I said in a quieter voice than Cassie and Tasha. I was surprised when Tasha smiled warmly at me in response and said "thank you" sincerely.

Cassie was the one who pulled her into a tight hug, speaking affirmations. "I knew you would get in, didn't I?"

"Yes, you kept saying not to doubt myself. Thank you for supporting me," Tasha replied.

"Anytime. Hey, we should celebrate!"

"Yes, totally," Tasha briefly looked towards me, "we could go to that pub we went to a while ago. Wasn't it called The Rozzen, with the z?"

"I remember that place. Yeah, we haven't been there for ages," Cassie said.

"So, it's settled. All three of us better cancel any plans for tomorrow night. Unless there was something important?"

The last question was mostly addressed to me as both girls had looked towards me. They had been trying to make it look natural but it wasn't working. I had begun to feel left out of the conversation, but I didn't think they would notice. I was stunned by the noise of the conversation for a moment.

"No, nothing important." It was nothing at all, actually, but they already seemed to feel sorry for me. Didn't want to give them more reason. "I'll just have to put that hot date on the backburner. Where is this 'Rozzen' place? Is it far?"

Cassie seemed to pick up on the joke while Tasha replied to my question. Cassie hit me lightly on the arm, smiling, before turning around to finish making the tea.

"I don't think it's too far from here. I can book a taxi tonight. We can go halfsies on that," Tasha was saying. She gasped as she looked out of the kitchen window to the morning sunlight. "Oh, I better get ready for work. I look like such a mess. I need to get a shower. Ah!" For the last exclamation, Tasha waved her hands in a dramatic motion before running back upstairs.

The kitchen was quiet again, and I could only stare at where Tasha was once stood. The toaster popped up.

Cassie was stirring a spoon in one of the mugs of tea. She handed me a cup as she gave me a soft smile. "Sorry about her. She can be... a lot. But you learn to love her. It's time to flip the toast."

I looked at Cassie, confused.

"You were making toast," she continued, pointing to the toaster.

"Right, thanks," I replied, moving back to the toaster.

"It's new for all of us, by the way, this whole flat share situation. It's all a bit weird right now. So, don't worry about it, alright? It'll all fit into place eventually."

I gave Cassie a nod. She left the kitchen taking a sip of her tea as she did so.


I couldn't help but be mesmerised as I watched Tasha on the phone to the taxi company. She seemed to speak with such ease, smiling often and calling the person on the other side "darling". I knew I couldn't be like that with a complete stranger. Forcing myself to look away at last, I went through my bag one more time. Keys, phone, purse. The essentials were there.

This was Saturday evening. I glanced over at Tasha briefly. She had dyed her hair the previous night and it was now a dark brown which suited her medium length blue dress. Cassie had appeared from upstairs. Her black hair was in a neat bun, and she was wearing a blue top with smart black trousers.

"You look nice, Cassie," I told her.

"Thank you, so do you, Sam," she replied.

I said thank you back, although I didn't think much about my outfit. It was just a black dress that my Mum had gotten me two birthdays ago. Tasha had gotten off the phone with a chirpy "you're a doll, have a great night".

Tasha noticed Cassie was in the room. "Cas! You look great. We totally need to get a picture together." She turned her phone to the camera as Cassie walked over to be in view of the phone screen.

"You too, Sam, get your butt over here!"

I couldn't help but laugh as I went over to them. I gave a smile as Tasha took a number of photographs of the three of us. I sat back down after the last photograph was taken.

"This is going to be so good. It's the first time we're all hanging out together. We should do this every Saturday."

Cassie had sounded less enthused. "Let's just get through this one first. I'm not sure I could deal with the extra Tasha energy on a night out more than once a fortnight."

Tasha mock-pouted. "Oh, but I love you so much. I don't give my Tasha energy to just anyone."

"I already need a drink," Cassie said, on her way to the kitchen.

"But I love you, Cas."

"Love you, too," was Cassie's muffled response behind the closed door of the kitchen, "You and your crazy energy."

Tasha turned her attention to me and sat down the couch next to me. She was less manic in the way that she spoke.

"I hope you're feeling alright about tonight. We can leave early if you get too uncomfortable."

"No, I'm feeling great," I said. It was surprisingly accurate to how I was feeling and I managed to give her a smile.

"I'm glad. I'm also glad you agreed to go out with us. I hope you don't mind me and Cassie's... energy, with each other. How many times have we said that word already? It's the last time, promise!"

"No, I love it. You certainly have a lot of vigour. Just to avoid the 'E'-word."

"Vigour! That's a great word."

"What's a great word?" Cassie asked, coming back from the kitchen. She was holding a glass of white wine.

"Sam taught me a new word just now. Vigour! To replace the overuse of the word energy around here."

Cassie took a sip from her glass. "Great, so now you can overuse that word while slurring your words tonight."

"Cheeky!" Tasha was going to say something else before she heard her phone beep. "Taxi will be here in two minutes."


I was the first one to open the taxi door as I heard Cassie and Tasha speak behind me. They were exchanging words about who had the key to the flat, and how the last time they went on a night out they had ended up calling a locksmith.

Sensing that they were not going to step further towards the taxi, I approached the taxi door first. I gave a nervous 'hello' to the driver as he asked where we were going.

"My flatmates are, err, leading the way," I blurted out awkwardly. I avoided the driver's reply to my stumbling speech as I opened the door again.

"Hey, Tash and Cass, shouldn't we be going?" I addressed them. I could feel the cold chill on my arm as I held the door open and was relieved when Tasha began walking to the taxi. I closed the door.

She and Cassie entered the taxi. Cassie was in the backseat next to me while Tasha took the front seat next to the driver. She was soon telling the driver our destination as well as chatting casually. Cassie interjected with comments once or twice.

I stared out of the window, watching the houses near our flat go by. I flinched at a sudden feeling on my wrist. I looked over to see that Cassie was lightly tapping me and looking at me.

"Hey, we're going to have a good night tonight," she said, "Don't worry about what Tasha said before; we're not going to be going out every week. We wouldn't do anything you feel uncomfortable doing."

I smiled at her. "Yeah, I know. I appreciate that. I am looking forward to seeing more of this town. And hanging out with you guys, of course."

"Good to hear. And you don't have to worry about us, just tell us to shut up if we're being annoying."

"I'm more worried about being a bore to you two."

"No, we love talking to you. I think me and Tasha just talk a lot because we've known each other a long time. But we'll become a three in no time."

The conversation ended there. Cassie and I sat quietly in the backseat, as Tasha was looking up the directions on her phone.

We didn't find the place we were heading towards. I heard Tasha alternate between complaining about the internet on her phone and apologizing to the taxi driver.

"You can just stop us here," she said, "I think I saw a pub down the road just now. I'm sorry for wasting your time."

"Are you sure? I don't want to leave you in an area you're not familiar—" the driver replied. His voice sounded patient and friendly.

"We'll be fine," Tasha interrupted. She softened her tone of voice immediately. "That sounded rude, I'm sorry. I meant that we'll be fine. And we can call for another taxi, at least we know where our flat is."

The driver tried to speak again, but Tasha was too busy with looking at the meter in the taxi. She gave the money over, and we quickly exited the taxi onto a residential street. The sky was already dark by this point in the evening, and I couldn't see any stars in the sky.

"Well, that was embarrassing," Tasha said, as we stood on the pavement. The driver gave us a wave goodbye as he drove away.

"What do we do now?" Cassie asked.

"We just need to walk around, there'll be a pub nearby. This is a student area." Tasha addressed me. "I'm sorry for the chaos, Sam. We usually plan a lot better than this."

Cassie scoffed under her breath, but didn't comment further.

"Okay, maybe not a lot better than this. But we can still have a fun night. And we can always try that Rozzen place another time," Tasha said.

"Hey, its fine. I suppose it's all part of the flat sharing experience, anyway. Plans going into disarray but it all turns out fine?" I replied.

I heard Cassie burst into laughter. "That's one way to looking at it. This is more like the experience of being friends with Tasha."

Tasha stayed quiet at Cassie's comment.

"Hey, it's not like I would have done better," I addressed Tasha, "we can find a place near here to get a drink and have a bit of fun."

She gave a decided nod at my remark. "Yeah. What are we doing standing here in the street? Shouldn't we get moving?"

The three of us began walking. Cassie was ahead of Tasha and I, seemingly leading the way. After a moment of walking, she looked behind her shoulder towards Tasha.

"Hey, you know I meant that in jest, right? The thing about being friends with you. I meant to say that you were like a ball of energy and we always end up having a good time on any night out," Cassie said.

"I know, don't worry," Tasha replied, "I think I am just a bit tired from work today. And I worry our driver might have got tired of hearing me talk so much, and how rude he must think I am."

"Nah, you were making conversation. You're just lovely and friendly. Anyone would love to have a chat with you. He was just looking out for us back there," Cassie said.

"Yeah, I guess he wasn't too bothered," Tasha replied. She took a deep breath and began to smile with more ease, as though a weight had been taken off her shoulders. She noticed me looking at her, and went to link arms with me.

"You were right before, Sam, this is just another part of the flat sharing experience. We're going to have a lot of fun times together, just you see," she said to me.


We found a pub after five minutes of walking. It was not too big building with two floors, which was painted brown on the outside. It was on a corner of the street, and the door in the middle had two sets of windows either side of it. There was lettering above one set of windows which spelled out 'PEACH SWIRLS'.

"That's a strange name," Cassie commented as we walked towards the door, "it sounds more like a beauty salon or something."

"Or a small crafting store, perhaps," Tasha replied, "anyway, does it matter what it is called? I thought we looking for a place to drink. There seems to be people in already."

"Yeah, I suppose it doesn't. I just thought it was weird. The name made me think of a painting in a gallery for some reason."

I had been adjusting my bag to make it more comfortable around my shoulder when I found myself being reminded of that dream that I had two days ago. The dream where I was in the white room and that weird man approached me.

"Sam? You coming in?" Tasha said. I pushed the image away from my mind and I followed her into the pub. It was just a weird dream. It didn't mean anything.

There were some people in the pub although not all the tables were filled up. Cassie announced to us that she would get the drinks in.

"Let's grab a table," Tasha said. I followed her as she walked further into the pub and eventually decided on a suitable table. It was a circular table which was placed next to pub bench, and a stool was placed on the other side of the table. Tasha sat gently onto the bench, placing her purse next to her. I slid my bag off my shoulder and sat next to her on the bench next to her, but I made sure not to sit too close.

"She's always been better than me," Tasha said. "At ordering drinks in a bar. I've tried to get the bartender's attention, but they just seem to ignore me."

"But you always seem so friendly," I replied.

She shrugged. "I guess I'm just not blonde enough. And I know I just dyed my hair brunette; I mean when it is natural. I shouldn't really be complaining about not getting guys' attention. I know Cas has had a few boyfriends. You know, sometimes I have thoughts about taking one of her exes. But that would be totally weird, right?"

"Perhaps. I don't think any guy has ever looked at me," I replied.

Tasha looked confused. "But I thought you said you had a date—ah, that was a joke, wasn't it? Sorry, I don't always catch these things."

"I didn't mean to trick you. I just didn't want you to think I had nothing to do tonight, like I was a boring person who didn't go out."

"We'd never think that," Tasha said, "look, you don't need to worry what we think of you. We're friends now. We'll stick together from now on."

I found myself smiling at Tasha's words, which she returned enthusiastically. I liked the sound of us being friends. I looked from Tasha's smile and noticed a figure approaching our table. Cassie had arrived with three drinks in her hand, two glasses of white wine and a glass of lemonade.

"I remembered you saying that you don't drink," she said, placing the lemonade in front of me.

"Thank you," I said, taking a sip out of the glass. I was going to comment further but I found that I was distracted by the way that Cassie was behaving. After placing the other two drinks on the table, she grabbed the stool on the other side of the table and sat at the table. However, she seemed more subdued when she spoke and kept glancing over to the bar which she had just came from.

I looked over to Tasha, but she had begun to speak excitedly about being out on a night out with her two favourite people in her life, and how she looked forward to many more.

"We should have a toast to that," she said, raising her glass up. I raised my glass as well. Cassie did the same although she still kept up her tendency of glancing back to the bar.

As Tasha took a long sip from her wine glass, she heard a noise from her jacket pocket. She took her phone out of the pocket and stood up from her seat.

"I better get this call. I'll only be a moment," she announced to us before stepping outside.

"Are you alright?" I asked Cassie. I had watched the front door of the pub close after Tasha's exit before eventually asking the question.

"Yes, I'm alright. Are you alright? We can go now if you want. In #fact, I was thinking of having a quiet night in after this. Yes—" she answered, speaking quickly.

"I was asking because you seemed nervous about something. Ever since you came back from the bar. I noticed you glancing over in that direction."

Cassie sighed in defeat. "Was it obvious?"

I leaned backwards so my back was on the couch. She looked sad all of a sudden. I hadn't meant to push so much. "I don't mean to put you on the spot—"

"No, you're right," Cassie replied, "I have been a bit uneasy. I saw a guy at the bar. He didn't do anything creepy or whatever. He just happened to be one of my boyfriends. Yes, one of them. I go out and meet guys, so what?"

"I didn't say anything like that. Although Tasha did say—"

"What did Tasha say?"

"Nothing. We were just talking about boyfriends and getting guys' attention. She didn't say anything mean about you, promise."

Cassie sighed in frustration. "I'm sorry, I know she wouldn't do that. I think I'm a bit frazzled because things didn't end well with this ex-boyfriend. That's the thing with dating sometimes; not all of them are as nice as you thought they were. Sorry to lay all that on you."

"Say what you need to," I replied, "I'm sorry you've not been treated well."

Cassie gave me a warm smile and patted me on the arm. "Don't worry about it, chick."

"When Tasha comes back, maybe we can leave here and get some chips or something," I offered.

"You don't mind leaving so soon?"

"Nah, I'm not fussed about that."

Cassie took a sip of her white wine just as Tasha came back though the door of the pub. She gave a quick apology for being gone. "Stupid marketers. I didn't know they worked so late," she grumbled. "What'd I miss?"

"We were thinking – well, Sam was thinking – that we could leave and go to a chippy," Cassie said, "I thought that maybe we could somewhere closer to the flat so we don't have to take a third taxi trip?"

"Yeah, that's a great idea. I've now just noticed how hungry I am," Tasha replied. She turned to me before continuing. "This wasn't too much for you, was it? Going out tonight? You can tell me."

"No, I'm fine. I just figured that it was good idea to get something to eat," I replied, "I appreciate you checking on me, though."

"Well, if you're so fine, maybe you won't mind paying for the chips?" Tasha teased, "I'm just messing. I can cover all three of us."

I smiled and finished the rest of my lemonade. "I just need to go the bathroom before we leave."

Tasha nodded as I heard Cassie ponder about the name of the pub. "I still wonder what 'PEACH SWIRLS' means…"


I enter the bathroom and I am surprised to see such a white room. The walls are white, as well as the stall doors and sink area. A contrast to the earthy brown of the pub.

I am about to go to the toilet when I notice a painting of peach and sunset swirls. It looks familiar.

I hear the door to the bathroom open and a man in a pristine suit, in his 60's, enters. It is the man from my weird dream. He repeats his line, as sincerely as he said it in my dream.

"How are you doing this fine day, young lady?"

I stand still, stunned by the man's appearance, when the lights shut off and the room begins to shake. The painting on the bathroom wall falls and hits me on the head, and I feel myself hit the ground.

# Untitled

By Bransha Gautier

# To My Father's Surgeon

By Tali Cohen Shabtai

I've realized how it
works: It is announced that ...
and it's known all of a sudden! *

You know that suddenness has
an action plan that is comprehensive
and detailed – it's
a strategy within itself.

When it (the suddenness) receives existence in a person's
ears
it is experienced as a malicious trick indeed it has no
advance warning or alert before taking
action.
Did you know that I had to
dismantle this trick
of suddenness

On the 27th day of January, 2015
on the 10th floor
of hearts in question marks
under full anesthesia
and full monitoring
            in waiting
very exact
for waiting for the
cardiology ward.

After all, the obvious suddenness
is no longer
understood
and has many consequences, it is the realization

that we are winning something that we
would not necessarily be entitled
to
        when
my father is on the operating table
at a supervised temperature
at which
you bypassed the blockage with an
additional route
in his heart

and I could not
offer you assurances
at this time
my father!

And/
I was to the Traveler's Prayer
and the chorus in the Book of Psalms, from "Blessed is the Man"
and to
the verse
"And all that he does will succeed."

Did you know
that I have connected to every special quality
for any trouble that may
come
obsessively?

And I was for every letter
of the letters of your name
in Psalms

and I searched for any mention in those hours
of heredity

Did you know that my father has three
daughters of wonderful Semitic beauty
will you recognize my father in them?
When you operated
with this suddenness on father.

And is charity not just a theological term
for gratitude
to be
considered –
please accept this (from me), surgeon!

*Heart bypass surgery, decided on within three days of detection!

# Nexus

By Bruce McRae

Momentous irony in lyrical passages.
Imminent transcendence.
Meridians of radiance in general concordance
with the what and the why and the where.

I'm writing a love song in cigarette ash.
It's like bejiggering a fly-button,
razzing the nexus, spinning on interwoven pinions.
A song about life ministering life,
about death pining itself to death,
a song of purgatorial evanescence.

Why so coy, feigning ignorance? This angular pretense,
you can cut the con, the aw shucks ma'am routine;
you know precisely what I'm saying –
that here is another song dripping in machismo,
oozing with *belle letters*, that's positively pulsating.
There's sex appeal all over its fingers and teats.
It's wringing with the fragrances of fallen angels.
A song containing massive physiological connotations.
Riding the nucleonic tidal bore.
Gyrating salaciously in the salient mainstream.

There's also impudence and impotence in equal shares.
And a disproportionate cheerfulness.
We're reconfiguring iambic preconceptions
before returning, eventually, to the source of our nature.
Like the undead, we're covered in taproots and lichen and
moss.
For ten thousand years we've been priming the soil.

# If the Heart Was A Trade Market, How Much Would Kindness Cost?

By Ololade Akinlabi Ige

In a filthy world greediness defiles the mind.
A boy hides his face behind some bruising walls
and a girl draws his dreams on the bed of stones.
Survival is an act of finding a home in broken houses.
Somehow, life is the dilution of happiness and sadness
but if fingers were equal, would God be forgotten?
Would trees' shades still be a home for indigents?
Yesterday, I embraced an orphan and renamed him
happiness.
Let's say the heart was a trade market, would kindness be too
exuberant?
I cut a portion of my smile for my neighbor because
happiness is the robe of the mind
because if I laugh while you cry, the world is not at symmetry.
This poem reminds me of my mum, of how expensive
kindness was when death sways her breath.

# Home Is Where The Word Is

By Dave Medd

Sounding down throat, heart, lung, bowel, groin,
her long, dark vowel of the soul rhymes
    with gnome and tome,
bubble and grub with worms in Eden's loam.

Word with ancestry and baggage. Tongue-
    thick, warrior word,
spoken through Beowulf's helmet lineage bronze,
rhyme-rich, chiming in hearth-light with harm.

A northern word for untold thousands of tears.
    Our best guess –
*haimi* – oiling her mouth with smiles,
or lovers, riding home on August straw.

Kids on yard in colliers' black fleck,
booting a tin can football over dialect's
    low brick wall.
These two, looping in lust, under hawthorn

shelters of sighs, on a heap they'll never reclaim.
Revellers, half-dressed, half-pissed, in light
    half-remembered,
*gannin hyem* to a leaf-ghost Viking bed.

This is her word, striving in stranger's earth,
    a borderland
thriving on outlaw fells where fugitives bark.
Her warm lips mouth on mine their mother's hum.

# Purple – after Mary Ruefle

By Shannon Frost Greenstein

After comes the
bittersweet remorse, viscous regret at the corners of your eyes
while you convince yourself
you'd be fine on your own.

After comes the
fallout, the wounds of the shrapnel of the voices of
anger that echoed under the clearing sky
as you clean the chickens.

After comes the
mud; the sticky, relentless, suffocating, futile
backdrop to every experience
the longer it rains.

After comes the
sadness, an ache, a blade through the xyphoid process
when you remember the early 2000s
and falling in love.

After comes the
damage control, frantic steps of triage by wartime medics
because your great-grandmother's china
is broken on the floor.

After comes the
rainbow, a prism of color and metaphor
you will not see because
everything is still mostly red.

# Humidity

By Tal Garmiza

This humidity
That takes you by the skin,
With everything that melts
And all things must be seeing.

Feels like a dream,
But not so much though,
Feeling everything,
Body - head to toe.

Would you like a drink?
Something cold for the blood
And soft for the dreams,
Take it easy on the skin.

The streets are empty now,
Like a feast to the brave,
Wait till evening comes,
when the colours are out to play.

And this humidity,
That takes you by the skin,
With everything that melts
And all things must be seeing.

# so i've been told

By Linda M. Crate

i don't know why we become ghosts when we're still alive,
maybe reaching out is terrifying but i would rather reach out
than to be left alone in this haunted house; i just don't
understand why my love isn't enough for some people when
it is intense and too much for others—all i really want is to
know why i must feel so much in a world where people seem
to feel so little? sometimes having a heart full of love is such
agony, it's not all sunshine and rainbows and unicorns as they
would lead you to believe; it is constantly questioning every
interaction & questioning every motive of every person in
your life—it is exhausting, you want to trust but you just can't
because the past doesn't work in your favor; but all you've
ever wanted was someone to understand—i want that, too,
and so i don't understand why i can't let you in or why you
can't let me in; but i hate standing outside this door with my
hand hovering over the bell—either i ring it and you reject
me or i ring it and we speak, i guess i fear your rejection;
because my love is intense or so i've been told.

# The Medusa Factor

By Jeanette Willert

Do you suppose we all have friendships
that sour as surely as buttermilk;
what was once cream risen to the top
turned?

So it was with us: delight
soured to animus.  And, so, we
lived out our last collegial years,
intense, at odds.

Years piled onto untidy years
since our unraveling— permitting me,
at the mention of her name,
to emit a disinterested yawn.

Then, she died—
younger than the norm.
And I am
confused
at the whoosh of loss
that flushes my veins.

A sadness seeps in
as I realize a Medusa
figures as largely in a life story
as any Eros, Pandora or Athena.

# Relationship Games

By Helga Gruendler-Schierloh

Is "romance," that tingly, dizzy, intoxicating condition that makes us see another person as larger than life, a web of unrealistic expectations and surrealistic images woven into the fabric of wishful thinking - or is it reality in its purest form?

In some ways, "to be in love" appears to be overrated as a nirvana-like state of bliss. All romantic entanglements, as glorified in movies, songs, and poetry seem to be at least to some extent motivated, instigated, pursued, and maintained by self-serving desires. It is a form of sweet "altruism" often preached and seldom practiced.

But then, could "friendship," a relationship that allows us to stretch beyond the monotonous soberness of everyday experiences, possibly promote deeper elements of truth? A five-letter word in English, an eight-letter word in German, a six-letter word in French, just to name a few, "truth" is of the essence for a healthy connection between people to last. Truthfulness seems to form the basis of friendship – or is friendship the foundation of honesty?

However, nowadays "friend" seems to be one of the most overused words in American English – as it has gradually taken on new connotations that go beyond its original meaning. The folks one generally meets at parties, business meetings, in the super market, and around the neighborhood used to be "acquaintances." However, the term "acquaintance" has all but vanished from the American vocabulary. And now we seem to consider, at least linguistically, everyone we get to know in a somewhat friendly (or sometimes even "not so friendly") fashion automatically "a friend." So, in current terminology "acquaintances" apparently have mutated into "friends" and the people we formerly called "friends" have evolved into "good friends."

Of course, the highest level of friendship culminates in the interaction of soul mates. Everyone knows what a soul mate is, right? Until you ask someone to describe it.

Maybe, like beauty, "soul mating" is in the eyes of the beholders, or in the hearts of the participants. It's a rare moment when two people noticing each her for the first time feel as if they have known each other forever, then walk away believing they have been brought together for a special purpose. Years of probing, wondering, and seeking instantly culminate in an eerie ambivalence of delightful fulfillment and subtle anxiety derived from the heady gratification of sensing one's own dreams and hopes in another, coupled with a subtle fear that this vision might burst and fold into nothing.

Relationships of romance, passion, and friendship can stand alone or overlap - with each new occurrence weaving another dazzling or confusing strand into the already baffling emotional fabric of human existence.

In order to comprehend the abstract it helps to visualize its evasiveness by projecting it onto concrete images:

"Romance" = a long-stemmed yellow rose, with glittering crystals of morning dew on its fragile petals to reflect the promises of the rising sun

"Passion" = a turbulent ride in a hot-air balloon soaring in a euphoric climb toward the possibility of extinction

"Friendship" = a fresh breeze on a hike through nature's evergreen miracles promising restoration and rejuvenation

Enticingly enthralling feelings can often be experienced at the start of a relationship when we are faced with a tempting smorgasbord of possibilities:

Eager absorption of compatibilities; cautious exploration of the unknown; anxious excitement about the limitless potential for things to be created; awe of a life force yet to take shape; and the almost irresistible desire to ignore the possibility that sometimes goals are unreachable, dreams fade away, and happiness evaporates.

There is so much to be explored: new, untouched, mysterious—just waiting to be found and embraced, with others, or alone.

Ultimately, we choose which game we like to play at any given time to satisfy our craving for human interaction.

# Untitled

By Bransha Gautier

# Burn
By Kelli J Gavin


I catch fire more often than I care to admit

I catch feelings that fan the flame

I wonder if others burn the way I do

I wonder if they have pulled all the alarms

You can only fuel the fire for so long

You can't watch from afar


I burn up rather quickly

My throat tightens

My hands wring

My eyes wince from the smoke

I wipe the soot from my skin

My feet tread carefully


Not sure where to turn

Not sure if the floor will hold

The beams crash around me

The flames shoot up each wall

Five alarm fire I am afraid

No one cares to respond


The flame is extinguished

Usually by me creating distance

The ruins are all I have left

The embers continue to smolder

Nothing will ever be the same

I don't have anything to cling to


It must be obvious

I sweep up the remnants

Nothing left to piece back together

At least the walls have been scrubbed

New rugs have been laid

All prepared for the next time I burn

# Time

By Jeffrey G. Delfin

If I could turn back the hands of time
For I don't want to lose you my sublime
I still remember the days when you are with me
Days I want to be forever with you if you let me be

Still reminiscing when we were happy
I thought our love is eternally
I regret the day when we part ways
I wish it didn't happen those gloomy days

Indescribable feeling, I felt
There were times that I want to melt
You are an angel in disguise
Being with you is like living in a paradise

How I wish you will be okay
Now that you are so far away
Memories of you still lingers in my mind
But I know there are things that cannot be rewind

Bringing back time would be impossible
The heartaches I've caused you is unforgivable
Forever you will always be in my heart
Even though I know there is someone else from the start

# The Unanswered Question

By Leo Lawrance James

They both, from a long time were waiting to sit together somewhere and talk. Talk to each other, sort out many things, express their emotions and get relieved. Clara and John were friends from a long time. They knew each other more intensely. They were everything else, but not lovers. John liked her and loved her too. But as she was in another relationship, she couldn't accept John's love. His sincere and devoted love had to be denied by her, but he never left his hope too. He hoped that someday, she would accept him. John though he had few girls who had approached him for starting a relationship, could never accept them, he could never like them nor could he love them because, it was on Clara whom he was determined into. Being with her, his eyes soothed, his mind settled and his heart comforted. Each time he saw her, he fell in love with her over and over again. They were far more than friends, holding each other's hands while walking, exchanging with each other the food they were having, drinking a juice with the same straw.

A couple of days ago, Clara had to conclude the relationship she was in. She quit it because she was unable to tolerate her lover's arrogance and possessiveness.

Since the breakup, Clara had been looking for an ideal time and space to discuss these concerns with John. Before when they used to be together, she would always talk to him about her worries in her relationship, but now she decided to inform him that she was free from all those complications.

Today was a fine day. They had finished their classes early and planned to meet near the chapel in their campus. Both, after their classes walked towards the chapel, reached the spot and found themselves comfortable to sit on a cement bench under a tree. It was around four p.m. in the evening, the scorching heat of the sun had lessened and it was sort of cool. They both sat there and were caressed by the mild, cool evening breeze. Clara untied her hair by removing the hairclip, groomed herself and retied it back. *"After a long time, we are sitting together"*, said John. *"Yeah"* replied Clara with a smile.

John: *Are you hungry?*

Clara: *No, No I feel, I had my lunch a little late today, just two hours ago, and I'm not hungry yet, but I'm thirsty, do you have some water.*

John pulled the bottle from his bag and passed it to her.

John: *You were not to be seen online yesterday, on WhatsApp. What happened? Evening, you spoke casually when I had called you to inquire about the assignments, but then we didn't have the usual chat at night, and I didn't even have your 'good night'. What's the matter?*

Clara: *Ahh. No. Nothing, I slept early. No, my phone was out of charge!*

John being very sensitive, knew Clara very well. Even the slightest lies that she said could be noticed by him. John held Clara 's hand gently and pinched her on it slightly. She stayed silent and was concentrated on a child that was walking into the chapel.

John: *Dear!*

Clara: *Mm*

John: *My dear! Tell me, what happened?*

John held her hand firmer and moved close to her.

Clara: *We broke up!*

John: *What? Who?*

Clara sighed.

Clara: *We broke up... me and Nitin broke up. Have I not said you about him?*

John: *Hmm. Oh, Hmm. Yeah you have. I do know him, through you.*

Clara: *mmm. Everything is over. I'm free now.*

John: *But what happened. Why did you break up?*

Clara: *I don't know John, we were very close to each other and I loved him so much. Though he was in Trivandrum, distance was not a problem amongst us. I used to call him daily, text him so often and cared him a lot. He was the love of my life and me too, his.*

John interrupted in between and asked, *"then why did you break up"*.

Clara continued: *There was something conflicting between us, even though we were lovers and loved each other, there was some form of friction in the flow of our love life. He always got frustrated over trivial matters and the relationship didn't go smoothly in many aspects.*

On hearing this, John grew upset, and sighed.

Clara: *I too am a reason for this separation. I was not satisfied with the way he loved me; I would always lament over tiny problems and get disappointed. So, the day before yesterday, for some reason, we had a fight. I called him later and tried to resolve the issue. But he was like, looking for a reason to end this relationship, and he easily said, "Let's end this now itself". And he also said that four years of his committed life with me was a disaster. More grief-stricken and desperate were all his days with me, he said. He was waiting for a reason to dump me,* and saying this, in anger Clara punched on the cement chair they sat.

John moved close to her and put his arms over her shoulder calming her.

Clara felt empty and was going to burst into tears at any moment, but she wasn't crying.

John: *Cool Clara. Everything will be alright.*

He didn't know what to tell her, how to console her and therefore remained confused and dumb.

Clara: *Yes, everything is fine now, I am alright. I slept to the fullest on these two days and managing to forget everything and I'm now recovering. Erasing the memories which we create, is a very stressful task.*

She put her hand over his neck and came close to him. With tears dripping from her eyes, she smiled at him. He got confused of whether those tears were of happiness or sadness, but then understood that it was a blend of both. He also smiled at her and was confused on seeing her blended expression. He too moved close to her and she could feel his breath on her face.

For some time, they sat in silence, both looking at the pigeons that nested on the roof of the chapel.

*"I have something for you"*, saying this John broke the silence, took his bag and took out three toffies from it. Clara was extremely excited and cheerful seeing them.

Clara: *hey…! Hurray…! Choki*

It was her favorite toffee. She grabbed it up from him, placed one in her mouth and began to chew.

John: *Toffee addict. Don't eat it alone, pass me one.*

Clara: *No, I won't.* Saying this she laughed aloud.

John chuckled as he saw her childlike behavior, and then they both laughed. John came close to her again and their arms touched each other's.

John: *I wanted to ask you something Clara.*

Clara: *Yep ask.*

Clara, chewing the toffee was looking at a sweeper sweeping the chapel. John was in a state of uncertainty on whether or not to question her. But she always gave him the freedom to talk about anything and everything. Bearing this in mind John chose to ask.

Clara: *Hey idiot ask, what were you up to. What's the matter? Will you please ask.*

John blushed.

John: *Clara, you once told me that you liked me, and you also told me that you would consider my proposal if you were not in another relationship. Now that, you've broken up and you're single and lonely, can't you now think of having me as your… may not be lover at first, but anything closer to it, can't you consider my suggestion at least? I'm not asking you to turn yourself on to me now and start loving me. But!*

Clara: *Hmm!*

She said nothing else but remained silent, keenly looking at the chapel and the sweeper sweeping and left John's question unanswered.

# The Ever-Unfolding

By Perla Kantarjian

in the likeness of all things
i find you.

see, you are as much ocean
as you are the curling of a strand of hair,
wave-like and stroking.

you are as much autumn
as you are the dawning of a feeling
at the touch of a fine sentence,
otherworldly and hallucinogenic.

throughout the uncreasing of my day
i carry you as though you are
shaped with the very matter
that composes thought.

and when night-time casts its liquid shade
upon my shoulders, i cascade into my pillow,
pupils wide open, eyelashes fluttering to your hymn,
remembering.

you held my hand under the moon
and for *days days days*
I could not wash the scent of
moonflowers off my stained fingertips.

# Love, What Art Thou? #9

By Yeshi Choden

I don't know what to call this
but this, I write for you
I remember how your face would contort
under discomfort and how your touch taught me
that love is nothing if not tender

but I remember them only as an indefinite feeling
that an old memory sometimes brings
leaving one nostalgic for what good can be recalled
and dazed by the lingering suggestion that
nothing really happened

many nights sleep with thoughts of you
and reproduce the past in dreams
but all my tomorrows belong to the days
I must live in pursuit of forgetting
with you, I had begun to understand what
it could mean to plunge into the abyss
where lovers dwell and incessantly die
without ever meeting death

you were the moon of all my skies
the likes of whom I knew would
make for lasting aches
you were the poetry
unveiled by silence
hanging over my heart
that writhed in quiet agony
to understand the parts of you
I refused to paint in colors of obscurity

what else is to have loved?

**In Love**

By Sumati Muniandy

Feel like returning to young age, rejoicing!
Puzzling, yes indeed...
Heart beat pounding, fire heating the surrounding
Jumping in joy, trying to close my eyes but can't get into deep slumber....
Something bothering me...
Waiting in anticipation...
My eyes searching for you love, with the silhouette of a single memory!
Days passing by slowly..
I think I am in love!
Looking forward to holding your hands
Walking towards the destiny
Life is to be lived, come on my love..
Paint me with your soft, tender touch
Looking for a shoulder to cry on...
You come into my life at the very crucial time
To fill the void
To complete my journey
Let's complete this life together
The phrase ' I love you' could never be enough...
Yes, I am in love again!

# Curtiss

By Douglas K Currier

He hadn't thought about Professor Curtiss in probably four years, Toby realized as he pulled out of the driveway. His 45-minute commute to work was beginning to lose its luster and he supposed that was what had gotten him thinking about Curtiss. Strange old duck, but much of what he'd told his classes over and over, like some sort of weird fortune-teller, or worse, some doomsday prophet, was coming true – at least in Toby's life.

Sequoia Valley had been fairly trippy anyway. Toby had been unable to get into a four-year school and hadn't had the money anyway, so the local community college had seemed to be the way to go. He'd kept his high school job at Subway and found himself in class that first day with Professor Sidney M. Curtiss.

Curtiss taught composition and eight or nine other subjects. Sequoia Valley – Fairdale was pretty much a one-man show – some office personnel, a few adjuncts in math, biology, other sciences, and Curtiss. He was hard to avoid and harder to miss. He addressed everyone by "Mister" and "Ms," always wore a jacket and tie, shined his own shoes, and said good morning and good afternoon to everyone as if it were part of his job. Curtiss' commute to the sleepy little community of Fairdale was over an hour from the nearest city, Naples, which might also have caused Toby to think of him.

Toby remembered the course description for developmental English, bonehead variety, that first day:

**Course Objectives:**

In Essentials of Effective Writing, we will review grammar and usage, punctuation, spelling, syntax, and mechanics – the vicissitudes of word choice and some of the foibles of the English language. In our writing we will pay close attention to the construction of sentences and paragraphs, and use these skills to write a series of short essays. We'll go over the correct use of written and copyrighted materials, as well as the ways we can incorporate such into our writing. We'll try to deal with some of the problems and misconceptions people often have about writing.

Overall, we will be engaged, both as a class and individually, in overcoming whatever obstacles each writer has – be they questions of process, technique, fundamentals, nerves – to being able to put words coherently on paper.

Lame. He remembered how Curtiss had gone on and on about writing – about how it was really thinking, about how difficult and important it was, about how it was key to opening human
potential, humanity.

At the time, Toby had pretty much let it roll off his back – much like most of what he'd heard in high school. He did, however, pause when Curtiss started talking about education, about how it wasn't meant to provide "good-paying" jobs, but how it was supposed to make them "human."

That had seemed a little harsh and looking around the room that first day, Toby could tell others weren't much in favor of being called "subhuman." In retrospect, however, Toby didn't figure that even that opinion, which Curtiss held right up until the end, warranted what had
happened to him.

For Toby, that's the way it began. Every morning commute, he found his thoughts wandering to Curtiss and his months at Sequoia Valley – the classes, the meetings, his classmates. He remembered all the classes he'd taken with Curtiss: composition classes, history, sociology, literature, psychology. It seemed like every semester there were at least two classes with the man that seemed the topic of conversation every day in the student lounge.

He remembered the time he'd ditched an advising appointment with Curtiss.

"I waited for you," he'd said. "What makes you think that my time is less valuable than yours?"

"I'm sorry. I didn't think it was a big deal."

"Well, it is a very big deal. I don't have the time to register you now."

"Can I make another appointment?"

"Why should I give you another appointment if you couldn't make the last one and couldn't take the time to let me know? What is the point of making appointments with you at all?"

Toby hadn't had an answer. Curtiss, from time to time, reminded him of his father. When his father had been home and sober, he would try to tell Toby about the ways adults did things. He recognized this tendency in Curtiss. Over time, he started to listen to him and sometimes even defend him to other students.

"I don't care what you say," Mike, Toby's best friend at school, said. Toby could almost hear him as he started the engine. "He always wants us to do more. He always wants us to 'want' to do more, and when we do what should be enough, what he's assigned us, he laughs at us and tells us we suck."

That was pretty much the complaint. Curtiss was too demanding; his standards were too high; it was only a community college for Christ's sake. Every day the suit, the tie, those glasses he peered over and played with, the questions that no one wanted to answer because there would only be another . . . and another – that was Curtiss.

It took Toby about three semesters to figure out that Curtiss was really seriously trying to help all of them evolve into useful people. He had stories. He was generous with his time. Those who weren't afraid of him could get a lot of help, but he was never easy.

Whenever thoughts of that time, that two and a half year relationship, came to mind at home, at work, with his wife, his friends, Toby put them aside for the commute. He rarely thought of anything on the way home from the job, but in the mornings he considered the problem of Curtiss. It became a game, a pastime – could he remember what the man had said and had he, from the point of view of Toby's current position in life, been right?

He considered what he'd known about the man: he had been around 60, his wife had died, he'd had no children, he liked living in the city. He berated students constantly for not being up on current events, was famous for telling them that being up on the news was what "adults do," a matter of responsibility to themselves and to the nation. Toby had had classmates who thought Curtiss completely crazy, who thought he did nothing but think of ways to make students feel like the inferior beasts Toby was coming to see that they were.

Some mornings, Toby thought that funny old Curtiss might actually, in some ways, be responsible for the person Toby was becoming. Certainly, his sense of responsibility had grown. He wouldn't have the job he had now, had it not. He understood perhaps some of Curtiss' frustration as now Toby had coworkers who couldn't manage to perform tasks either well or on-time. He sometimes heard Curtiss in his own speech to others – moments when he corrected his own grammar, moments when he was aware of fallacies in the logic of others. He sometimes heard his father as well – but those were mostly obscenities. One morning he remembered Lila.

Lila. Toby hadn't paid much attention to her at first. Mildly attractive in a sort of available, townie way, she was not one he placed from high school. She'd started at "Sequoia Valley" during his final semester. He'd only Sociology with Curtiss. She was in the class. He came to know about her almost casually – had a kid, worked at Walmart, relatives in the area, high school somewhere downstate. The unkind things – that she'd fucked her way through the staff at her last job, that she'd fuck almost anyone if she could get something out of it, that she never pulled the shades in the little house she'd rented outside of town and liked to walk around undressed. Well, Toby had tried not to listen to too much of that. He knew that in towns the size of Fairdale people said lots of unkind things just to amuse themselves. Toby was trying to rise above the town and his place in it. At that point he'd been applying himself for a while – saving some money, refraining from the evening six-pack, eating better, doing homework, and, more than anything else – listening to Curtiss. He'd figured out that in all of the different classes he'd taken from him, the old duck hadn't been making up the shit he said. Curtiss had pretty consistent opinions on education and responsibility and could support them. It had gotten so Toby felt that class with Professor Curtiss *was* higher education – regardless of the subject.

This meant simply that he'd excused himself from the student lounge bull sessions and concentrated on his studies. When students bitched about Curtiss, he merely smiled and nodded, refusing to rise to the fever pitch of perceived injustice or even to defend the man. Things might have worked out much differently that semester if Lila hadn't come to town, hadn't enrolled in school, hadn't registered for Sociology.

Lila hated Professor Curtiss. She knew she hated him – his suits, his ties, his shoes. She hated that Curtiss was distant, somehow above his students – maybe even his colleagues. She could tell – all that calling people by their last names, all that proper, respectful, fucking distant language.

Lila didn't know it, of course, but she hated any man who didn't physically want her. She didn't feel safe around such men. High school had been easy. It was easy to flirt with the male teachers. She'd ignored the females. Mr. Hendricks, the assistant principle, had liked her a lot. Whenever one of the bitches, like Ms. Small, gave her a hard time for her clothes, her tattoos, she could sit in his office and feel good about the way he looked at her.

She couldn't get Curtiss to look at her at all. He would ask her in that tight-ass way if she'd done the reading. He'd lecture all of them on the importance of knowing what was happening in the world and applying to events the 'sociological perspective.' He never leered at her the way the boys in class did or the way Mr. Hendricks had.

She tried. She mostly wore thong underwear. She

had a nice, compact ass, if smallish breasts. She didn't wear a bra much, preferring tight shirts that featured her normally hard little nipples. She made it a point to sit in the front row in class, but Curtiss seemed to take no notice of what she wore. He would sometimes comment on the general lack of taste and propriety in student dress, but never seemed to notice, peering over his reading glasses, what she was or wasn't wearing.

One morning, after trimming her pubic hair the night before, she'd come to class in a tight skirt and no underwear. She'd sat in front, as usual, but periodically spread her knees in a random, nonchalant way, crossing her legs over and over to see if she could get Curtiss to notice.

She'd been pretty sure he'd seen her cunt; she'd done her best – scootching down in the awkward school desk to give him a better angle – God knows everyone else in class knew what was going on – but he'd given no sign, no indication, mentioned nothing.

She hated him even more after that, if that were even possible. She became sure that Curtiss hated her as well, although Lila mostly interpreted indifference as hatred. She also had Curtiss for English Composition I. Sociology, she was pretty sure she could do enough reading to get through, but Composition was too much work.

Toby noticed the feud between Lila and Curtiss, if that is what it could be said to be, about mid-semester. He wasn't in Composition, having taken it earlier in his career at Sequoia Valley, but he heard Lila talking to anyone who would listen every day – mostly the male students who hung out in the student lounge – and he had begun to watch her reactions in Sociology. Professor Curtiss would, of course, ignore the unseemly spectacle of clothing and flesh, Toby knew him well enough, he thought, to understand that Curtiss would see all that as beneath his notice. When Lila started spreading the rumor that Curtiss was gay, Toby began to watch the two more closely.

While not beautiful, or even exceptionally pretty, Lila was desirable – emanating a sexuality, a need, made all the stronger by the professor's indifference to it. It was not lost, however, on the other males at the school. Typically, she'd fuck a guy for a couple of weeks, then move on. Initially, she did townies – men and boys who wouldn't ever be going to school: town crew, bar flies, high school boys, but into the semester, she started dating classmates – the lounge flies to whom she complained constantly about Curtiss. There was a rumor that she'd done an adjunct instructor, but Toby never actually knew that for a fact.

The next morning on the way to work, Davey popped into Toby's memory of that time. Lila had finally found Davey. Davey was new that semester as well, but shared no classes with her. He had Curtiss, however, for Basic Writing – that remedial writing class for those who'd just barely made it out of high school. He was bewildered by the amount of work. He understood little of what the professor said, depending on attendance to get him through, much as he had in high school.

Toby remembered the day he'd happened upon them in the lounge on one of the sofas. Lila had had a throw pillow on her lap and Davey's left hand fumbling and burrowing between her thighs. Toby had turned around to leave when Lila offered the explanation that the student was "trying to warm up his poor hands."

For Toby, it seemed to come to a head after the Easter recess. The snow was slowly going. Spring seemed a distant possibility and the semester was ending. He'd been in to see Curtiss a couple of times: once to register for graduation, another time to discuss transferring to a four-year college. The professor was always very supportive, and Toby realized that the man's support was simply contingent on the younger man's desire to advance, or as Curtis would have it, evolve.

"It's not too soon to contact the state school if that's where you want to go. You have decent grades, so they'll be happy to hear from you there,"       Curtiss had said to him. "No one can want this for you. Obviously, you have to want it for yourself, and the degree is useless if you don't actually learn anything."

It was always like that. Toby liked to think, when he was sitting in front of the professor's desk in the dingy, windowless office in the school's basement, that what Curtiss was telling him was more than just the advice he gave to all students. It might have been his imagination, but Toby thought Curtiss might have cared a little bit about what happened to him.

After Easter, however, everything changed. Toby got the story second or third hand, but he saw its effect on Professor Curtiss.

Davey told the story to anyone who would listen, but Lila must have told him to.

Thursday afternoon. Lila had made an appointment for some help in composition with Professor Curtis in his office. Once the door had closed and Curtiss had sat down behind his
desk, Lila began to disrobe. She'd come with that in mind, so she was perhaps wearing less
than usual – t-shirt, skirt, sandals – deceptively demur.

As soon as she'd pulled the t-shirt over her head, exposing her small, high breasts, her erect nipples, Curtiss stood up behind his desk and asked her to leave. Lila responded, "You don't want me to leave this way, do you?" and pushed down her skirt, revealing a very small thong. As she stepped out of the skirt, she said, "I'm not sure I should have to get naked just to get some help on my paper. What will people say?" She knocked on the door of the office, and Davey opened it, using his I-phone to film Lila and the professor as Lila squirmed out of the thong and dropped it on the professor's desk. "So if I let you hold onto this," she said, sitting on the edge of the desk and spreading her legs as if she were in a porn shoot, "you'll give me some help with my paper? Excuse me, Professor Sidney M. Curtiss of Sequoia Valley Community College, but that seems a little perverted. I'm sorry, but I won't fuck you, even for an "A," you old pervert. I have to leave now." She then reportedly, slipped her clothes back on, minus the thong which lay like a poisonous snake on Curtiss' desk blotter, and left with Davey and the I-phone. Apparently it had been her I-phone, but the result was the same.

The next morning, heat blasting for the early cold, Toby tried to remember how he'd first heard of the incident. When pressed, Davey hadn't been able to remember the professor's response – something about Lila's being sorry in the future . . . something, something about that sort of thing being beneath her . . . something, something, it saddened him . . . something, something. Davey thought getting to film naked Lila and the old letch professor was pretty hot, but no one could see the film – maybe later. Lila had a plan.

Curtiss never spoke of the incident to Toby, and Toby was pretty certain the professor spoke of it to no one.

He imagined the professor had said how Lila might regret the behavior for the rest of her life, how such a thing was beneath a young woman with potential enough to be a student and to seek an education. Curtiss seemed sadder after that – not worried, not preoccupied, just sadder, and almost imperceptibly gentler with his students, at least in Sociology.

It was still cold enough some mornings to cause Toby to let the old car warm up a little before taking off, to huddle, blowing on his fingers while waiting for the engine temperature to reach a level where the heat blower would not just be blowing a strong, cold draft in his face.
He sat there thinking whether or not it had been Davey – the way he'd come to understand the notion, the motivation, behind Lila's strip that afternoon. Davey had had a good run, but even after she'd moved on from doing him, he continued to be a co-conspirator, sniffing around,
whining, hoping she would fuck him again.

Apparently Curtiss was to give Lila at least a B in both Composition and Sociology if he didn't want the video made public. Toby had wondered about what school officials at the main campus in Waterford would think of that. He was pretty sure it would look like the amateurish, frame-job it was. Curtiss had been at the college for years without a complaint of that sort that Toby had heard of. The professor didn't act like a man worried about his job or his reputation at the school. Toby remembered asking Davey if Lila really thought that would work, if she thought anyone would believe that old Professor Curtiss actually traded sex for grades. Davey had said no. The idea was not to give the video to the school, but to post it on the internet. Both Davey and Lila were sure it would go viral –

there would be investigations on the state, maybe national level, if the old fuck were stupid enough not to give Lila the grades she deserved.

Toby had tried to talk to Professor Curtiss about the situation, the blackmail. After class, after everyone had left, Toby broached the subject:

"Mr. Donnelly, so you're almost finished, well on your way to making a life for yourself."

"Professor Curtiss, I wanted to talk to you about what I heard about this thing with Ms. Lawson."

"Mr. Donnelly, you don't really expect me to discuss your classmates with you. That would be extremely unprofessional," Curtis never used the word 'inappropriate.' For him, courtesy and professionalism were moral qualities. "You needn't worry about anything aside from keeping up your work through the end of the semester. Graduation is no excuse for slacking. Your next institution of higher education will expect the same, if not more, from you."

"I was just worried. I didn't know if you needed something."

"Ah Mr. Donnelly, I've been around for a long time and seen almost everything, and I'm still here – not turned to a pile of salt, nor struck blind, nor burst into flame. I expect to hear good things of you. I expect you to succeed in your endeavors and that you'll eventually decide what those are. Remember, quiz Thursday."

And that had been it. The semester ended – final papers, final exams, all of which always seemed due in the same week. Toby hadn't attended graduation. For one thing, it was always held on the main campus in Waterford – a place that meant nothing to him – on a Friday. He'd have had to take off from work, and he'd come to think of it

348

as a piece of paper. He remembered his high school graduation – so much joy and high seriousness – leading to drinking and nothing more but life. As Curtiss had said to them many times, the completion of anything – project, degree, course – was not a signal to stop, but an opportunity to prepare for what came next. He'd gone straight into summer classes at the state school, wanting out of Subway immediately, and to make up time.

New, larger city, new school, new job, new people, it wasn't until a year later that Toby heard of the fatal car accident involving Professor Curtiss. Apparently, from what the newspaper had said at the time, the professor was involved in a single-car accident on his commute home from school – Route 16. He'd been wearing a seatbelt; he hadn't been drinking, and it had been a clear, spring evening around dusk. There was speculation that he'd fallen asleep at the wheel or that he'd suffered some sort of physical anomaly – stroke, heart attack – something. He had been pretty old, after all.

Toby thought from time to time, especially when he was commuting to work, that Professor Curtiss might have died of sadness or of weariness from working with students who seemed to have no limits, no values, no ambition. He thought it might have been like that.

Years later, he'd met up with Lila. She'd graduated finally, not from Sequoia Valley, but from a different community college, with a dental hygiene certificate. She'd changed some, but not enough. He'd found her working as a receptionist for a dental group in a building not far from his work. They'd arranged to have coffee. When asked what grades she'd received from Curtiss that spring semester, she'd had to think a minute: "A 'D' in composition and a 'C-' in

Sociology. The son-of-a-bitch delayed my graduation an entire semester. I had to take both over at the next school just to get into the hygienist program."

"I thought the fix was in."

"Shit. By the time I got my grades, the old fart had died in that car accident, so I never posted the video. I had to give a copy to Davey to shut him up, but he knows if I ever see it online, he's dead meat."

Six months after that conversation, he'd married her. Her daughter, Gillian, was great – a really smart, precocious 10-year-old. Lila was coming along. Turned out, Toby thought to himself, often on the commute home, she'd only needed a man who wanted her and could tell her 'no.' He felt responsible, not for anything or anyone in particular, just responsible to the world – something he thought Professor Curtiss might have understood.

# Revival

By Eva Eliav

George ate the same meal for dinner every night: grilled filet mignon, a small portion hardly larger than a demitasse, but the best quality meat, very juicy, his knife sliding through it as if through butter. The thick chunk had to be medium rare, seared dark on the outside, pink in the middle. Placed beside it was a baked potato cooked in silver foil for about an hour then split and adorned with a sprinkling of salt and pepper. A green salad – cucumber, lettuce, tomatoes, garnished with slivers of onion – was served in a wooden bowl beside his plate. The bowl, kept especially for George's salad, looked like half a coconut rubbed smooth and stripped of its creamy flesh. George liked to read the paper while he ate, and Susan made sure he wasn't disturbed. She'd always been a very attentive wife. Though George never commented on that fact, Susan felt he knew it and was grateful.

I might as well confess George was my dad. He was one of those dads who rushed in after work, swept up his kids and hugged them, then hurriedly went off to live his life. We met him during the evening only by chance. That was home: the rush, the kiss, the smell of grilling meat, the paper brought neatly folded then spread open, taking over a large part of the table. Later, sounding far off, the TV news. And very late, if I was still awake, the muffled clangs of boxing matches father loved to watch.

Sometimes, I'd slip out of my room and peer into the den. There dad sat, upright and alert, hands curled into fists, duplicating moves. The glass of tea my mother always brought stood cloudy and untouched on a nearby table. I gazed for a few moments, then crept away.

My mother was in bed. Fast asleep. She never stayed up past ten. A bit of reading, then the light went out. Though my parents' rituals were worlds apart, I was convinced of their loyalty and affection.

I was in my twenties, living on my own in another city, the day I made the call. My father answered. Cheerfully, I asked him how they were. "Talk to your mother," he said. Then he was gone and my mother's voice was saying, "We're divorcing."

I don't remember more of that conversation. Only those two fragments, and then nothing.

Life moved on. My dad found another woman, many women. My mother married again. Each lived in a new place, my father's functional, my mother's cozy. Once they split, I rarely saw my father. My mother had been the glue that held us together.

I try to forget the past. Or at least to view it through a misty lens.

I've bungled it. What I'm experiencing now is a resurrection: the rush, the kiss, the smell of grilling meat, the salad gleaming red and green as gems, the TV murmuring in another room. Father's throwing punches, alert, intent. Mother's asleep, hands tucked beneath her cheek, her hair still thick and dark, her body young.

I'm longing to see them but the house is cold. Soon even my father will have gone to bed. I burrow under the covers. It can wait. Everything will be here in the morning.

# Lily Pad

By Rachel Makinson

I noticed a blossom petal, falling through the bleak spring air.
Its pink skin grew transparent as it was dissolved into the
damp rusted metal of the train tracks. Supplemental petals,
that mattered much less, tumbled down beside, around, and
on top of my petal — some helplessly melting into the wet
metal also, whilst others lay fresh and still very much-alive on
the gravel. As the train huffed into the station most of those
little petals, including mine, were of course macerated
beneath the monumental weight of the wheels. I picked up
my luggage, two scuffed and outdated cases, and I boarded.

It was a long journey, and the tediosity of it all was
exacerbated both by uncomfortable seating, and by the
lingering fog that occluded from my eye passing scenes of the
English countryside that I had ached for months to see again.

Dear Aunt Emma was there waiting for me at the station,
with my cousin Richard who I had only met on three other
occasions, all when I was very young. Being five years my
senior, he remembered me and my silly childish antics well,
but I could barely have recalled the colour of his hair. In turn,
they each hugged me, and I climbed into the back of their
swish, very new looking, automobile as Richard hauled my
cases in beside me.

"Hold on tight to those—" he said. "Bit of a bumpy ride."

In my memory, Aunt Emma's hair was a warm honey tone.
But the years had taken their toll on my poor, dear Aunty and

time had dyed her hair the colour of chalk. She was the youngest of the sisters. Aunt Charlotte was the eldest; my darling Mother the middle child. The past years had been cruel to all of us, but Aunt Emma had suffered prematurely. Her daughter and husband were taken from her just two years apart, and before the war had had chance to even begin its destruction. I think after all of that grief and all of that suffering, a head full of silvery hairs at one year from fifty was more than justifiable.

The car crunched up the driveway, and we came to a gentle halt. Aunt Emma's house was modest in size, certainly by comparison to Uncle Rufus and Aunt Charlotte's house, where I had had a bedroom, bathroom, drawing room and sitting room all to myself for the past four years. But Aunt Emma's house was much more endearing to me. I was charmed by the honeysuckle, the little apple orchard, the fish pond with its water flowers and stepping stones. When you crossed them, you could peer down at your reflection, and made it ten times more beautiful than it was in any mirror.

Our house in England had been in Norfolk, by the coast. Even when it was much too cold, my parents, Frederick, Pippa the Spaniel and I would take a picnic down to the shore. Sometimes Frederick and Father, if they could find wood dry enough, would make a little campfire to keep us all warm, and we'd toast marshmallows and sandwich crusts in what would usually be rather pathetic little flames. Still, it was fun.

It feels both as though an infinite amount of time stands between now and those memories, and then again, it feels, fallaciously so, that if I were to stretch my hand out far enough, I might be able to intercept my Mother's hand as she reaches to take another scotch egg from the picnic hamper, and hold it in mine, for a little while longer. She always smelt of Bergamot. Sometimes I venture up to perfume counters just to smell her again.

There was a writing desk and a fireplace in my new bedroom. I could tell the maid had only just lit it. The room still had a vacant chill to it. There was an en suite bathroom too, with a large bathtub. Aunt Emma had filled the shelf beneath the mirror with lots of lovely things: bath oils, sweetly scented soaps, face creams, perfumes — all unopened and unused.

"I imagine you'll be tired after such a long journey. I would love to visit Charlotte again, but I think the trip over to America would be too much for me these days. Well — we'll let you rest a while, Lillian, before dinner. Would you like Martha to bring you up anything to eat in the meantime?"

I smiled, and shook my head.

Aunt Emma wrapped her arms around me and squeezed my heart close to hers, "you be sure to get plenty of rest now. Rest and the countryside will make you feel right as rain in no time."

\*\*\*

I remember those first few weeks at Aunt Emma's well. After I rested that afternoon, they served me a dinner of hot beef, creamed potatoes, and mixed vegetables followed by a slice of cherry tart that obscured most of the plate it was presented. That was the first and only meal I managed to finish for a very long time.

I remember the walks — around the garden, around the orchard, around the village. Around and around. I cried as we passed the memorial for the first time, rooted there in the centre of the village green. It was piled high with fresh flowers; crimson poppies, tulips, daffodils, sweet peas, bright blue delphinium; whatever people had managed to crop from their gardens, or otherwise get their hands on. Aunt Emma passed me a handkerchief, and pressed at her own eyes with another.

"They're watching over us, Dear", she whispered. She squeezed my hand.

I remember old Mr Fitzpatrick looking me up and down as we bought bread from his bakery. I remember Mrs Lewin's weak smile as she shook my hand. I remember how Miss Riches and Miss Hewitt whispered about me as we left the post office.

I remember going to the seaside and walking through the harbour with my cousin, putting on my best pretence that I was enjoying myself, and that all was well. We ate lobster in a divine little restaurant that overlooked the bay and we took a stroll up along the cliffs, gazing at all the different seabirds through Richard's binoculars. He was an avid birdwatcher. I tried my best not to seem bored, or paranoid that the birds might be watching me as intently as I was watching them.

I remember the doctor shining a torch into my eyeballs and taking my temperature. I remember him pulling a little leather bound notebook from his pocket, and scribbling down pages after pages of notes as I spoke to him. I remember the look on Aunt Emma's face as he led her out of the room, and I remember the pitiful little smile she gave me as her eye caught mine.

And then I don't remember. Not well.

*

I sit in a wasteland. There is nothing personal about this room, no stories to be told — other than that of the sick woman who once resided here. She was lost in her own lunacy.

I pull at my hair, and a tuft falls loose. I am twenty-eight years old now. I am childless and unmarried. It was my birthday yesterday.

"*Tick-tock*" — says the clock.

Look at her. Such a frightful reflection. Her skin the colour of bones, her cheeks hollow, her eyes bulging like the belly of a pregnant pig. They used to say I was pretty, but now I am a ghastly sight. A bizarre, iniquitous creature.

"*Tick-tock. Tick-tock.*"

Martha comes in with a tray of tea for me, and toast that she knows I will not touch. She smiles and asks if there is anything else she can get me. She is a pretty thing. Surely no older than
seventeen.

*"Tick-tock. Tick-tock."*

The steam and sweet scent of lavender is calming. I stir the hot, soapy water with my yellow-grey fingertips. I take off my dressing gown and sink into the water, its warmth washing over me like an embrace. I close my eyes. Everything is calm, momentarily. I slowly submerge my shoulders, then my neck, then my entire head. I hold my breath a while.

The water is murky from all the soap. I begin to swim. Up and up and up. I take in a gasp of bitter cold air and I smile. The water is serene now. A little robin lands on a buoy that bobs just yards from me, its sweet melodious voice accompanying the soft crashing of sleepy waves. I swim to the shore and fall back on the golden, velvety sands and watch as the school children finish their weekly swimming lesson; all ten of them in their little yellow rubber swim caps and red and white striped costumes. They all turn, in unison, and wave to me.

I move away from the beach, scraping the sand from my legs. I wear the same swimming costume as the children, but the cap has fallen from my head as I swam to the shore. There is a little path that I follow. It leads me up into the meadow. The grass is tall and thick, and tickles the tops of my bare feet and legs as I creep through towards the misshapen trunk of a silver birch. I run my fingertips along its branches, pull at its flaking bark. I pull and pull until all that is left is a sad little twig that one of the children from the swim school must have stuck there. Perhaps it marks buried treasure.

"Oh, Lillian! Whatever are we going to do with you?" Aunt Emma bustles towards me. "Leave it be, let it grow!" She carries a wicker basket full of freshly baked iced buns from Mr Fitzpatrick's bakery. "Richard's going to drive you down to Salcombe tomorrow. That's where he sails. There's a lovely little restaurant he's going to take you to."

"I don't want to sail, Aunt Emma."

"Of course not, sailing is a man's sport really, isn't it? Let's go home and sit in the garden. Fresh air is the cure."

I don't want to sit out in the garden, but we sit there anyway. Aunt Emma wraps a tartan wool blanket around my shoulders. It itches at my neck but I cannot remove it without her tutting and readjusting it about me.

*"Fresh air is the cure."*

The maids bring out an unpalatable selection of food: beef-jelly sandwiches, tomato sandwiches, sliced pears, deviled-eggs, mixed nuts, a large fruit cake and a pot of tea. The eggs are eyes, staring up at me from their silver plate. I think they know. *These eggs know everything.*

"Do eat up, Dear. You *must* eat something. Isn't this fresh air wonderful!

"They're watching me, Aunty."

"Who, Darling?"

"The eggs, Aunty. They're watching me."

She laughs, then her smile drops. A frown. Sadness.
Sympathy.

"Perhaps you're a little sleep deprived, Dear. Why don't I take
you up to your bedroom, for a little, post-luncheon nap?"
I nod. I nod. I smile. She takes my hand in hers. She squeezes
it. Together, still hand in hand, we walk inside.

The heavy heels of her boots clomp against the hard oak
floor. My cheeks are burning and my stomach twists.
Everyone knows we're coming. Everyone knows we're here.

The post office smells of mothballs. What use can there be
for mothballs in a post office? Perhaps it's the old lady
working behind the desk. I imagine that after I have lived for
a further forty odd years, I will probably smell of mothballs
too, or something similarly disagreeable.

I go up to the elderly lady and hand her my parcel. She places
it upon the scales and looks up at me.

"What are you posting today, Dear?"

"A birthday present" I say, "for my brother."

"How lovely." There's a smirk beneath her smile. "An American address! Were you raised there?"

I push a coin in her direction and turn to leave.

*"Mam! Your change? I've got your change here, Mam!"*

I crawl into bed with a pad of paper and a box of pencils, and I draw a face. There are delicate lips and a petite nose, sharp cheekbones and elegant eyebrows, but no eyes. This woman will have no eyes. She will be beautiful.

There's a clatter at the window. I look up — a magpie, scratching its talons against the glass. I fling open the window, to scare it away. It's all alone, settling now on a frosted branch.

The snow is falling again. The flakes spiral down onto the bare skin of my arms like imps. My feet crunch with each step I take, like on a pebbled beach. *They are watching me.* I close my eyes for a moment. My breath is escaping me. The air is so cold that it's weightless, without energy or vitality. My toes and fingers are numb, my body quaking from its own weight. I scratch the tears away from my cheeks in fear of them freezing over. There's blood on my fingers.

Mr Fitzpatrick approaches from the bakery, with a coat draped over his right arm. There are others still inside, peeping out at me from the window. I cannot tell how many they are; the longer I look the more faces appear. More and more and *more.* All of them watching.

"Here take this — Miss Harris, are you unwell? Shall I phone for the doctor?"

*** 

They thought my recovery miraculous, but what miracle is there in a mind becoming tired of its own cruel games and fantasies? I was only set free of them only for a little while. It was less than three months before I found myself back in a hospital bed. But in that time, I moved myself back over to America, to visit Frederick and his wife, Sarah. We had fun together, riding and drinking and throwing parties almost every night. Then I moved on to New York, but it wasn't all that I'd dreamt of.

I bought an apartment of my own with the inheritance from my parents. Aunt Emma had warned me that moving back to a city, and on my own, would be a terrible mistake. She was right. I would have died there, alone in that sad apartment if it hadn't been for Marigold, the little Papillion I had bought to keep me company. As I lay passed out on the floor one night, she yapped and yapped until our neighbour finally came to complain, and found me. I think she probably just wanted feeding.

I went back to live with Frederick and Sarah for a few months then. And again, I recovered. This time for much longer. I married a wonderful French Canadian named Lucien, and together we had a beautiful little boy who we named Robert, after my Pappa. Lucien was a brilliant father and a splendid husband, but he never did understand. I suppose, really, that even I did not understand how my mind would dip in and out of insanity like a biscuit dunked in and out of tea, edging closer, with each dunk, to total collapsation. Nor did I understand how my little Bobby grew to contain the same sick mind as my own. I had tried so hard to raise him well, but this madness — it was infectious. After a decade or so, the realisation that I had contaminated my only child was inescapable.

I would hear him, mumbling to himself in the same way that I would sometimes catch myself doing. I would hear him cry at night — scream even. I would catch him staring and laughing at random objects. He went through a phase with the Welsh dresser —whenever his eyes fell upon it, he was captivated, transported, almost, to another world.

It was like watching myself — as though the healthy part of my soul had back jumped from the sick, and stood, helplessly observing. I never said a word to Lucien. I didn't want him to realise, too, that I had ruined our boy. I didn't want them to take him from me. The very thought of losing him brings the taste of bile up into my throat.

Bobby sits with me now. He reads Carroll's *Jabberwocky* as I write. I reach my hand out to my boy, cruelly cutting in on his little escape. His fingertips feel warm against mine.

"Mamar", he says. "Do you suppose there are many others out there like us?"

# There is Home In Our Wounds

By Ololade Akinlabi Ige

How leaves unfetter from trees reminds
me of the scars in my spine. This poem
is a mortician carrying home another
memory. I envelope myself into grief
to join the echelons of mourners around here.

Tonight the wind breaks us into ululation
and we sail home memory in swarming coffin.
My father serves us chalice of regrets,
this, with parcels of condolence satiate us with hope.

Silence spins around this room and my mother's
monochrome thumps on the wall.
I grope over my wound and pleasure steams out from my
pains.
That I smile doesn't mean I am not burning,
hope is the feathers of the mind.

I once held a bird and called it my mother's name.
There is no light where I found home,
that is to say darkness lodges in my heart,
that is to say my body shields bleeding sky,
that is to say I am a half moon.

Yet I define everything as happiness.
I chose life the day my tears tasted salty.
There is melody in the lyrics of dirge,
I mean there is a home in our wounds.

# Satellite TV

By Jude Brigley

# A Movie List Poem

By Bill Cushing

I've lived life in celluloid, marking time mostly

by movies that immersed me in worlds, real or ghostly.

Casablanca taught me the true manly art,

watching Rick come alive through Humphrey Bogart,

but the first to separate film from a movie

was delving into the breadth of Westside Story.

Warrior-filled epics like El Cid may focus on men,

but the true star—to my young eyes: Sophia Loren.

Star Wars, at first sitting, marked a sci-fi breakthrough,

returning to basics but still brand new.

The ultimate sensory deep-dive, Apocalypse Now,

blends sight and sound, a blood-soaked Pink Floyd show.

Admiration of Paddy Chayefsky

took me to Altered States, which brought me

to William Hurt who then let me meet

Kathleen Turner by way of Body Heat.

Apologies to Private Ryan, but Das Boot's a better view

of battles and military life in World War II.

Last of the Mohicans, the film Michael Mann was born to make,

took a boring novel and made it great.

I recalled youthful fears with Apollo 13,

while it allowed me to peek behind the scenes.

LA Confidential, Chinatown's cinematic cousin, took

the podium as a movie that beat the book.

Cooking and film make a great combination;

then Chef's added ingredient connected a father and son.

Lately Hell or High Water carried on tradition

by giving us a modern Western.

When the story of the doughboys had to be told

Peter Jackson showed us how They Shall Not Grow Old.

While there've been no previews so far

of life lessons in fantasy or lodestar,

wherever life, film, and I now go,

I hope to have the best seats, center row.

# Kayla for Stasis

By Shaista Fazal

The line snaked across three city blocks. People had braved the rain and cold and stood for hours in line to get a chance at the screening. A small square entrance portal defined the point where the line seemed to be headed. As each candidate came near it, the entryway slid up and when they entered it dropped down shutting the rest of the crowd out. The building housing the eliminations was huge and windowless. A great hum emanated from it; it was the noise made by the hundreds of cooling machines required to keep the structure cool.

Kayla stood in the steadily moving queue and sighed, it was cold and wet and the wait was seemingly unending. She was hungry and her feet hurt, but her heart was full of hope, and that gave her the energy to buckle up and keep standing. She watched as several people eventually gave up and dropped out of the line.

The line kept on inching forward and soon Kayla was near the entrance. "Just a few more candidates to go and then I will be safe", she thought. Just then her pager beeped. Startled, she huddled deeper into her parka. "Oh God, the tracker in my pager will lead them here in no time at all. Please hurry, hurry hurry."

She muttered under her breath.

To her immense relief the portal opened and she jumped in with alacrity. The guard standing just inside smiled at her knowingly. With a thought sensor strapped to his head he could easily sense her mental vibrations. The invention of the thought sensor in the last decade had done away with lots of cumbersome security measures. If one could sense the thoughts of the person in front, then one could take action based on them. A simple easy innovation!

Kayla smiled back and hurried on, down the long winding corridor.

A smile of relief lit up her face, at last she was safe. Now she only had to pass the elimination round. She had worked really hard to get all the paperwork done, it had involved a lot of running around different departments to get her documents in top shape.

As she neared the end of the corridor a round opening slid open and she slipped inside. The room was lined with chairs filled with people waiting their turn at the eliminations. Kayla sat down and awaited her turn.

She was here to undergo the preparation for 'Stasis'.

Stasis was a slowing down of the body processes and of the bodily fluids, a sort of hibernation period but not seasonal. You could choose to be in Stasis for either one or two centuries according to the program you selected. It took a week for the body to be prepared for this procedure. A painful process it taxed both mind and body to its limits. Only the tough of body and mind were able to endure the full procedure. Many gave up halfway; but there was a catch! If anyone gave up halfway they were as good as dead as they had to spend whatever life they had left like a pickled vegetable!

Then why were so many people committing to being in Stasis? Why were they choosing stagnation over life and living? What was driving them to this point?

The answer lay in the present day conditions here on Earth. Earth had been totally spoilt for life. Pollution had done away with most of nature and its fauna and flora. Great barren deserts now covered vast areas of the planet; where once beautiful forests and magnificent lakes had been. Blue skies had been replaced by grey murky ones. Most of the food now had to be grown artificially and was tasteless. Only the rich could afford foods with enhanced taste and the chemicals used to do that were killing them off.

After centuries of searching for worlds which were more habitable than the home planet, humanity had come to realize that there was none to be found. Humans would have to make do with the one planet they had in hand. There was no other better world to flee to!

Armies of "Climate Warriors" had then been formed around the world and Earth was being terraformed on a war footing. However scientists had predicted that it would take the world at least a century to revert back to normal. Meanwhile the conditions here on Earth were becoming hellish and unbearable to live in. There was a universal uproar amongst the masses and a clamour to find a way.

Beleaguered governments across the world had agreed to work together and come up with a solution; and the solution was "Stasis". When people were put into Stasis they went into a state of suspended limbo from which they could be awakened at a pre-decided time and by applying another procedure. People could stay in this state for decades or even centuries, making it an ideal escape route from the current world crisis.

The Stasis procedure had been invented a few decades ago and was legalized by some countries. But it was so expensive, only the very rich could afford it at first. However in the past decade the climatic conditions on Earth had deteriorated so much that people were desperate to escape them in any way possible. Now the Stasis program had been made accessible to the common people through government funding programs. It offered a beacon of hope for those brave enough to attempt its painful process.

What were the advantages of going in for Stasis?

Entering the program required a long and tedious vetting process. You had to be medically certified by a panel doctor that you were in good physical and mental condition. You should be free of any pending legal issues and also free of debt. You should have a good credit score. And most importantly you should have a no objection certificate from your immediate family.

Then began the week-long procedure of painful injections loaded with drugs to preserve the body in a static state. The mental processes were slowly shut down with psychotropic drugs. Then The comatose body was placed in a self sustaining nuclear powered capsule. The capsule was self sustaining and required no external maintenance. The capsule was then transferred to deep underground vaults where it would stay for centuries if required. When the time came for the reawakening of the human inside the capsule, then again a long process was undertaken to reverse the stasis.

So why was Kayla here? Young, energetic and beautiful she had her whole life before her. Why was she choosing to be a vegetable instead of being a vibrant living form?

Kayla's mind went over all the events of the past year that had culminated in bringing her here to this room. A year ago she had been a mother to a 5 year old son and wife to a loving husband and so happy. But that was all about to change with the advent of the Stasis program. As soon as the program was announced, she noticed a change in her devoted husband. He seemed to be aloof and moody. When Kayla questioned him, he explained that he was going to register the three of them for the Stasis. Kayla was shocked! Why did he want to do that and that too without her consent? Did he not know about the risks involved? And what about their son? Will he be able to endure the procedure? What if one of them did not make it?

But he was adamant and registered himself and their son on the sly. He even forged Kayla's consent letter. When she returned from a two day business trip she found her husband gone and her son with him. She was dealt a double whammy when she realized that she was now saddled with their joint debts.

It took a week of running around and cutting through a lot of bureaucratic red tape to find out the details of what had happened. Her husband was one of the first one to apply for the Stasis program along with their son. He knew that Kayla was opposed to the program and feared for her son's safety, but he himself had complete faith in it. He believed that if he went into Stasis for a century or so then he and his family would awaken in a much better world as had been promised by the scientists.

When Kayla vehemently opposed him, he decided to go ahead without her knowledge, and take his son with him. He took out a loan to finance the preparations he needed to get himself and his son to get declared medically fit for the Stasis. He even pulled some official strings to get his son admitted to the program.

The result was a bereft Kayla who was left searching frantically for her family. It was at this point that she made the decision to follow her husband and son into Stasis. She desperately wanted to be there for her son when he woke up. Then she realized she would have to clear the debts left behind by her husband if she wanted to enter the program, and this seemed impossible. Luckily for her when her boss came to know about her story he agreed to help her by calling on some favors a powerful official owed him. This enabled Kayla to enrol for the Stasis. But at the last minute just before she was to reach the Stasis center, her debt fraud was discovered. Somehow she managed to flee her captors and once inside the center she was safe and immune according to the law.

So now she found herself sitting in a chair waiting for the interview, which would determine her eligibility for Stasis. An official emerged from the door and beckoned Kayla in. she entered a small boxed up room to face the questions that would determine her fate.

"Why do you want to undergo Stasis at the prime of your life? You have your whole life before you" the official asked.

"I love my son and I will follow him to eternity to be with him and be there for him. He was taken away from my arms to sleep for a hundred years and I, as his mother, want to be there when he wakes up and cries for his mummy."

"Permission granted," said the official with a smile.

# Stairs

By Jude Brigley

# Watching Jordan's Fall

By A Whittenberg

... God, I hate November
All the hope I had hoped
Against hope for Jordan.

Dad beat Jordan, to
Straighten him out, to show
Jordan, to silence him.

My brother lived until the next
Season, onto the next winter,
Very quiet like a fallen leaf.

# Mother Earth
By Jeffrey G. Delfin

Killing me softly,
Though I cared for you faithfully
Is that the way things it should be?
I thought this bond will last between you and me

I gave you everything that you need,
I am always there for you indeed,
I am your source when you need food,
Truly an example that I can do good

I gave you Trees that provides shelter,
To make your living comfortable and better,
Sun that gives you energy everyday,
To do your task each night and day

Unpolluted air to make you alive,
To be able to make you survive,
These are some of the things that I can offer,
If you will destroy me, many will suffer

Please protect me and let me live,
Forever your needs I vouch to give,
I hope that you will love me back,
I will be your provider and that is my pact

# I Chew Poetry

By Peniel Gifted

I chew poetry with my meek mouth
Invocating despotic words untold
I wonder if they are infallibly words of old
Invocating words never to be abashed

What does me
If I keep hiding the flavor
Of my unending crystal whor
That speaks aloud the love of the unheard prodigy.

Oh mother of Earth, give me the poetic drink
A million times
I need eating from your table
Of this beautiful words from Niles

Poetry, my Poetry
As mild as a moonlight
Poetry, the bird of peace
As Cupid, you keep my heart so buoyant.

With my incredible poetry
Surely the world must be blazed
Beholding wonders, the quaternary race
I'll keep chewing with my meek mouth
For In my blood stream lies the healing pills of poetry..

# Fallen Leaves

By Thomas Zampino

It's not as if I can count them all.

Each drop of rain striking hard, like a bullet against the first
of the autumn's fallen leaves, and gravity ceding control to
the already soaked ground just below.

Some leaves seem to have completely given up, pinned down
by the weight of their own wetness. Others scatter freely,
unable to resist the forces still cutting through them. As if
caught up in some kind of mechanical afterlife, first pushing
forward and then quickly circling back.

The teeming, rancid earth now readies itself for animation
and annihilation, both, whichever first cares to overtake it —
flexibility and complacency remaining, as they are, essential to
an unstated recognition of life's fullness and of its betrayals.

But soon enough the rain will stop and I'll doubtless forget
just why any of it ever mattered.

# Untitled

By Guilherme Bortoluzzi

# Sometimes

By Tal Garmiza

Sometimes
my words
leave me
defenseless;
I am exposed
to the naked eye
and I feel naked
inside.

Sometimes
my words
leave me.

# In Memory of Lost Birds

By Ololade Akinlabi Ige

and when repeatedly reciting

my mother's last words,

i curated a melodious dirge.

in this dark room

i am finding my lost self.

every day, i fight memories i cannot win

& i seek God's face in broken mirror.

i do not know how my scars grow into a country.

i mean, i do not know how my hope

turned to a heap of dust.

i am moulding again everything i lost

& i put away my mother, sister and the girl

that taught me love- they are lost birds

that do not know the way home.

# Seven Impossible Things Before Sleep

By Ruchira Mandal

Holding hands at the beach, promising eternity
As we lie on our backs, counting the stars.
We will carry on from where we left of tomorrow.
There is always tomorrow.
Watch a star crash, and make a wish
On the ashes of a planet dead eons ago.
Trace our names on the sand.
Hold the sea at our feet,
Though we only catch the clinging sand.
We wait for the next wave.
Tomorrow, we shall return to the world
And the birds will sing.

# Sidewalk Crows

By Anannya Dasgupta

# Becoming Rain

By Lorraine Caputo

The evening rain

Became the pre-dawn rain
A woman sweeping the cobbled streets
        clean of Saturday night's revelry

Became the morning rain
Dimming the western mountains
        the jungle river valleys
Sketching a rainbow above
        the misted green

## Of Time And Mind
By Bruce McRae


The rain turns back, a slick-footed messenger.

The rain mutters something under its breath.

The rain. Its small furies. Its night-blessed auguries.

Countless mirrors are breaking over a curb,

pewter bells, cymbals of heft and velocity,

bantam pipes skirling in the arbutus' branches,

like glassy-eyed fairies skipping in the garden.

The rain can only fall, everything *down*,

everything under its wheels and heels.

The rain at night, grey unto grey.

Making landfall. Strident. Uninhibited.

Rewriting summer's epistle, repeating its chorus.

Rain, with nowhere to cower or hide.

That's pouring out its farthings and dimes.

Silver spurs. Grey eyes. Obsidian sweat-drops.

October rain in the wee hours,

alien *clang* from the dockyards,

a scent of leaf-fall and wet earth,

a seaplane's *basso profundo* growling

over a darkling sea . . .


Morning's littlest uprising,

so much to be written and read,

clouds mirthlessly knocking noggins,

streetlights reflecting, deflecting, diffused,

the firmament's porcelain a belated orange,

an odd light betwixt post-midnight and pre-dawn,

darkness merely hinting at darkness,

daybreak in the next room rehearsing its lines,

a play in verse, words biting into the page

before leaping into that broiling inferno

of time, place and mind.


One has to ask: Is this all of what there is?

The lackluster music of room temperature.

Moments dissembling, then reassembling,

a harsh light between sleeps . . .

One is forced to ask, what hurts?

What moves under night?

Is there still an above and a below?

Questions asking other questions . . .


Glib with history, a distant siren replies.

# Creatures of Nature

By By Anannya Dasgupta

# Linger A Bit Longer

By Thomas Zampino

As the days compress,

And light makes quick work of its retreat,

As fall begins its fated descent,

Reminders abound that our hours are numbered,

And only One knows the time, the place, the reason.

That uncertainty is the only given,

Grants us permission,

To seize each day, or even just a moment,

And to linger a bit longer within it.

Exchanging clenched fists,

For the touch of another's hand.

Surrendering ourselves completely,

And thereby finding life.

# Baked Hedgehog

By Dave Medd


Twenty stone of monolith, whopping barrel-belly,

they called him Durham Bob in Seaton Sluice.

Grey jowls, saggy sacks that shook in scowls and quarrels;

round as an o, scarified, sculleried face;

eye pin sapphires; hair like frost skeins;

a name to craft alien status north of the Tyne.


Sang as a boy in his cathedral choir

(better at whistling now in the club's hot fume,

driving comrades mad with impish joy).

Brown paper under his vest kept winters warm,

a parcel of wheezes. Bragged like an old myth's bear,

steeling apprentices with a fistful of roar.


He could quote the rule book line for line, bonny lad,

keep committee secretaries straight;

lit seam and shaft with language and lamp.

Once, when snow was mindless, turning white

all hope of work, trudged four miles, to keep

the pit wheel grinding up tradition's heap.


Should have drunk less; beer flushed out his dreams.

They found him once, near death, in long dune grass

collapsed, a savage comedy of forms.

Fancied girls and pigeons by the gross.

Indefensible. Unreconstructed. Didn't

hold with bloody swearing in front of women.


Pit crippled arm he cradled like a sick child to his heart.

Needed a hand with his coat, and that was a privilege

of sorts. Grey sea niggled through the cut

and washed old bottles from the fisher's vantage.

He declared best Yorkshire puddings need pigeons' eggs;

best poacher, knew the best butcher; he could bake

hedgehogs.

# Bridge

By Jude Brigley

# Step to the Bridge Nous Delphica

By AE Reiff

The top worlds drawn on the bottom are three or four times as large in the middle. The number of colonies is 183, not counting suspicious invisibles at opposition. After the original 79, the majority north of the equator, 116 were not on first maps of either the dark regions or the light. All these sites had connections to tunnels below from the above ground. These tunnels reached to both coasts. When it came out that they were camouflaged as krill plants on the ocean competing with the whales this enabled them to make the celebrated bagoong. Large slabs stuck up out of ocean to drive the krill, which were larger than expected by the little people who worked them, if that can be said without profiling. They were not from anywhere exactly or anybody is. Mornings in the corkscrew. Some exceptions from a loss of surface occurred within the spirals.

I am not squandering words. We pray on Sunday for those at sea.

Those shrinks who cleanse Newtown and the effigy of Achilles Arch spread the myth that this colony has wings of cloud and fire. If so, we advise shooting those birds before they land. Leviathan Bay or LevBy sounds like Long Island off Montauk. When the Sun rises all wild Beasts hide themselves in their Holes. In the event of this *vaticinium ex eventu*, prophecy after the fact, history written as though it were prophecy, the old world was dying so new monsters grew. The thing about tentacles that reach through land and sea is they mimic pattern DNA. For more on this study **Thoughts from Singing Birds**, the paranoia mon amour that surrounds Alternative 3 of the Dictates.

*We don't mean whales here, for Maria pseudo-hirsuta* was evolving. The eyes look west with dragon heads. Zillyzation needed Long Necks for this humor. Waiting to appear that Hydra seemed alive with moving heads, tongues lashing. Bigger than blue whales but invisible. Contoured and finned, masked and tusked, metallic surfaces scaled like a head of that state, reptilian don musk, Leviathan Pharaoh. Which is all mythological nonsense anyway? Is it beast government produced out of oil and gas, one of four beasts that come up from the sea, drilled and mined? Dragon mines the elements. Dragon crews for dragon gas. Such a state is liberty to those who measure their freedom by the subjection of others.

A female has vertical eyeballs like a frog which the international community must undertake every possible effort to end. "The shapeshifting capabilities of organism 46-B shaped itself into the form of a human diver. A 33 foot-long man-eater of extraordinary camouflage stalked our researchers. It disabled our radio, which we later learned, to our alarm, was intentional. "It is also able to paralyze prey from a distance of up to 150 feet by releasing its venom into the water. "Tragically my colleague and lifelong friend was killed this way. He tread water wearing a blissful smile as the organism approached him. Terror is a joint effort by *Dante I*, an eight legged tethered robot.

To obscure its mythic name in the Leviathan community

Who dares call it swimming in this Casanova's Colon? The epath of Leviathan of thrust faults and under land seizes, under, beneath, Behemoth above ↕ prospected by earth and under sea is news to any who imagine it swimming up aquifers and getting fracked. Creatures in a river impose on ourselves a temple that feels no sides. There is no freedom between yards of blubber imprisoned by events. Unaware of its own Leviathan movement, states and individuals swim in opposite directions without knowing. What is freedom when compelled one way by current while swimming as fast as it can in the other? Read the scientific papers on genetic machines, the last greatest covering globe. Scrutinists in this way show their absence. RockaBilloy history makes it a victim. Miners need our protection.

**Leviathan** has a greater following than Behemoth among these mystics. They make necklaces out of the scales. The brazen fins of wanton whales suggest other political types too, as do the shark teeth scattered over beaches. If a mouse could climb through an elephant's trunk to gnaw its brain, then a whole town country planet can be undermined by the proboscises of leviathaniasis. And whether Beo takes LevBy withal, to wear its spectacles, nose piercing through the snares within the ribs where dolphins swim, the mighty body falls.

King over the children of pride those sperm dress alike, ready to disperse such organs as the most rebellious body parts of Adam shamed. *Illa parte magis regnat additamentum leviathan* spawns abound in *Janus,* Luther or Mamet, prisoner or flesh, and lead all other parts to rebel beside water and on land. As serpents gripe and break the hot petcock from our sight, moving land and under sea, remember that banquet to be served. ⧻Behemoth *Apatosaurus* or *Argentinosaurus.*

These were the torturers among our legislators and senators, those burgers of consensus: who had rigid views of identifying common ground and crafting strong consensus. It only remained for them to blur the last definition, what is the human. Could that air head speak it would say that the colonist like a mouse is meant by the Armed Forces to be an experiment to save itself.

2. Pantheon gods inaugurate in Water. At Old Town Leviathan-by-the-Sea, the  picture is of a creature who boils the depths out of its mouth. Old Town has credentials therefore both as the **Temple of  Neptune and the port of**

**Noah.** Global romantics in Rome are not surprised that Nous Delphia is Troy. The horse enters the city. The city is burned. if Neptune hid the horse what hides in these? They call it a Trojan Priest who threw his spear against the Old Town polity of gods. One global temple of distortion, like some universe emperor of the despond kingdom who says all is well with ziv, even its discontent, until it's not. Sea serpents against. Figs as dates, dry head that cracks shall be lawful for any Athenian. Geologics spin over every proportion and property of the place. Figures swimming overboard can be seen under waves after ships have sailed as if they loose an anchor snared on a reef This presumes a vacant mind. upon this strange color with something of their own, pretty sure to approve. We might expect to meet a certain person, or an approaching figure that deceitfully took on his garb. The mere idea of this walking image makes an expectation to endow it with the attributes of a friend. This may happen truly as well as false. Mind familiars act.A very slight hint from the eye goes a long way in the brain of one naked, and no distance at all in the brain of the other. Ship channels dug into rivers like the Hudson enable Lev's passage further and further inland. Some covert arrangement seems to exist between ship channel captains and administrators of Leviathan and Co., meaning the fish itself. Why not call it a fish or a reptile of some sort which cooperates with the dredging to continue that progress started by bodies jetting up and down the rivers to zoom through glacial canyons miles out to sea. This churning happens as if there were racing and makes for weird weathers of mist inland on both sides, for there is more than one, else how do they breed, but leave that to the entomologists.

Speaking as the spirit of unknowing that human mind disports, if passage tombs could talk, or under bark organics and rock, volcanic ash, erosion deposition, reburied feldspar, fish streams under clay spines, would they dare say *more* than they heard? What they heard was ascribed beast government, four empires up from sea. The first a lion with eagle wings, lifted on two feet, like a man with a human heart, forfeitures of British Royal Lion and American Eagle with all democratic pretense. The second was a bear with three ribs in its mouth, Russia chomping the Baltic down. The third a leopard with four heads and chicken wings on its back, Germany and its Nazi survivals surmounted with France's national bird: the French army knife that came with a white flag. But the fourth beast unlike them all had no nation but covered the world, a beast for everyone that calls it fracking, fragging. The Baptists have a name for it in their Afligidos.

♥Archuleta is a case in point, not only land. Five caves honeycomb it and plenty of other visibles from the peaks do not reveal the *magnificenza* to be discovered under water. Those who keep their heads and chests above the tide of transverberation like some brute dolphins plunge the cliff-sheltered bay equivocate eye and wave together. Simple rectilinear, curvilinear pi, the mind sees, not the eye has tributaries to it.

**As unsatisfactory an explanation** as this is, and as impossible to comprehend, these warring parties occupied the waters and waterways of Nous Delphi. There is a further complication, that being that the account here is a translation from notes taken as these ideas unfolded, patch worked together, often with arbitrary custom, often being simply the last one that occurred, and then further condensed, as if the attempt were to achieve a kind of verbal alchemy, parts of words broken off, neologisms, other languages, homonyms substituted for nouns in an old century baroque style. It has been the custom for writers to pretend to be editors for some time, so it may not be entirely believed that this story really is a translation even if from the English. Why does English need to be translated from English? Simply because the original writing is unanimously judged incomprehensible and samples could readily be offered, there being above a hundred pages, but we fear that would only cause one to put down this account. Suffice it that this is part history, part mythology and that it has a didactic end implied withal, but figuring that out is a little beyond what the translator fairly believes should be attempted.

Mabinog colonists down by the water, hang with their backs to the land and gaze out to sea, the poems of Kiss embossed in holograms behind them at Dulce Port. They sit on jetties, reverie on Ocean Inhaesio, extasis, seeking the thing, not the thing's reason. Too new upon the land to even carry succubi in their hands, eyes open on keypads while their ears hear the roar, they wait in the smell of salt for leviathan. Think that sculptors and the piscine shapes of women know what goes? How many fishes in the deep blue sea? What's the cause of simplicity in priests? The dilemmatic and problematic structure of virtue.

Of course leviathan undersea is curves and planes, as Heraclitus its prophet said, but on its surface, ever changing, *nothing to be seen but storm between the clouds and waves, a cataract of fire that rose and sank again in the scaly folded crest above the waves. It reared on golden rocks in globes of fire, eyes that evaporated sea in smoke. Leviathan's forehead divided green & purple streaks, a tiger, its mouth and gills hung wide. Just above the illuminations of blood and foam was the fury of a spiritual existence advancing.*

Eternal Father, strong to save, protect us from the restless wave. O hear us when we cry to Thee For those in peril on the sea.

Unchangeable or changeable in position, the colonies gradually emerge for some reason inherent in themselves, conspicuous with the visible development of the canali following the melting of the snow. Only when such melting has progressed can the colonies be seen, as if the moisture invigorates their air. For instance, our colony darkens considerably about eight miles up the Pisinemo Road near KiaHoaToak. Near Carrying Basket Mountain, known for its horsehair and yucca, beargrass, and martynia, come the tests of bathythermograph. hitty pitty within the wall.

When stone hits glass the breakage conforms to gravity and glass and reason covers her breasts. Only the tension in the freedom to act and crack unknowing reveals the submerged. Yes that is a little simple. Crack the stone, conceal the stone, railroad ties connote forced labor, famine stone denotes starvation and slavery. Of course I wept, tears ran from my eyes as if I were burning wood to make charcoal. of the mind where Dedalus heated onions in a pan. If these firings were apocalypses, then the pine would die in the fire! Believe that and read the Great Wall as a kiln opening that asks, what is the seventh seal? I hate to spoil the ending. Round as an apple, deep as a cup. The most peculiar case is the Ulysses, the other face of Judecca, of strange riddles in steady air, that put to rest natural causation. The regularity of the caves, uniform width, their systematic radiation exceeds any ordinary natural contrivance. What they are not helps to decipher what they are.

So if it can be borne that this tale is true, partly true, built out of truth and facts, but at the same time false in that the geography, the people, and exists only in the ether of someone's mind or fantasy, it is a lot like our lives. Enjambment maybe is its reason for being, an analogy of ourselves in transition between this world and the next, caught in forces we know little about but think we do. So as they used to say when the ships pulled in, or in the modern sense if you are caught by INS in a good mood at the airport, Welcome to Antarctica. Further likenesses of old and new occur in that the old was refuge from persecution of the European for those whose beliefs got them tortured and killed. Colonists fleeing persecution for its own sake brought their afflictions with them. It's always government and religion that people flee, and government can cover a multitude of sins, and religion. Freedom from these was the purpose of refuge, which should account suspicion on government. But while pilgrims in their fall from grace into grace have much to share with the pietist pilgrims olds, they do not share the externalization of hierarchy. Living in two worlds at once, *overtly* in the spiritual and physical they did not see directly into the spiritual as was required in the New. All the back places emerged and the robber as friend, was a nice way of saying the Adversary took all these forms in the physical and spiritual, but so also did the Friend. We use these euphemisms to soften the blow once vision has lifted.

To drink up a river, snort Jordan up its nose when the sun has seven times parched the whitened foam that gives up its beasts and falls to the whirlpool throat, interwoven and fused in the devoured and devouring world, and goats stomp stars and then the fourth beast, diverse from the others, whose teeth of iron and nails of brass devour and breaks in pieces all residue under its feet, where the other three were slain, even if they had their lives prolonged for a season, then Gabriel takes orders to end this indignation. A vision of daily sacrifice where the transgression of desolation gives both sanctuary and host to be trodden under foot. When these four winds of heaven blow it is time to sail, to take thee to ship on the tossing sea.

It does reveal clues only you can find, then follows as if it knew where you were going, or where you were, should you be going. Individuals in that state bow down. A commonwealth is free to invade its own. It wants to be caught sneaking up behind. That's the freedom universe! Where people rule the subject slave.

**The only exception** to these dives below the surface seeking contact, soft kill, slow kill, silent kill, the perfect beast to cull the herd, synthetic telepathy, psi tech, Smirnoff patent, programmable black metal, or clams and oysters for delicacies, Leviathan is never seen in the harbors by its devotees and invitees who are all the more attentive to make up costumes for Lev Day. They Snake Dance through streets and practice frenzies as if it were not enough that they live in Leviathan homes and wear Leviathan clothes, worship the universe as children of pride what they have not seen, well rarely. Leviathan causes the depths to boil and out of his mouth go sparks of fire and burning torches. The picture is of a creature whose passing causes upheaval. Now look at Behemoth: "If a river rages, he is not alarmed; He is confident, though Jordan rushes to his mouth."

If you yourself live between the cultures of myth in the aquarium humane, Ossian on the grass, Pythagoras, Plotinus, do not grudge to find the same soul of the world in land and water, Behemoth and Leviathan. There is a herd of Behemoth upland, not the Nazi auroch transplants that escaped after GMO. More than reconstituted mastodons, this does not account the hulk landslides. Spotted and browned, earth into mine tailings and shards of dirt and rock, then tramp up the thousand mountains to forage trees. Behemoth has no natural enemies there unless you count lightning. Neither does it breed says myth, as if one only waits to meet its mate in leviathan. Higher up the lightning strikes are more frequent than polyploided escapes from labs, rats as big as cars, coyotes as big as parking garages. A sapling catches fire, hisses and drips and a thorn bush whoosh. Visible invisible combine in the colonies, if one can speak of managing Behemoth.

DNA altered genealogies, lists of foods, strange government camps, Blackbox and Red Rovers. universal surveillance state the digital version of every telephone call made to, from and within the U.S. since 2005 but to really get to the bottom to the infinite hydra head we go to Lake Volstok **Then came a time when the stone cats envisaged faery heads upon us.**

Tidal influence at Old Town reaches pretty far inland. Old Dame trots out some cold fish she got. Elders swing their censers as lamps. In the water light wolf to cub, curvilinear pi, the mind sees not the eye. The standoff between draggle and pickled pig intersperses submerged ruins with dreams, Antarctic voyages waking unconscious from the ground. I'd never seen a ship that sailed that wide. In the temples, labs and board room foreheads Ezekiel saw the visions of Elohim. Galloping Galloway, Rhetors of Neptune, look at your neck; there you will find the strap.

**It's hard to locate** settlements the dolphin mire among zephers. The new looks like the old. That government required ship lists and oaths of allegiance, when harbor sea captains began to slump over their water jars. Some believed they were living in the Odyssey of Homer and sought the madness of the sea joined by pietists in the settling of New Delphia, complete theologies of severance among themselves. Settlers are conscious of their mythological status.. The future trails in the present, then becomes the past. This kind of recurrency recurs again. New Delphia occupied a harbor like Rio, but in the north. These made space for their rituals in the harbor and along the beaches looking down from bluffs like the coasts of Catterline and Prouts Neck, slump shouldered sea mounts, white snow hills in the air. Swear by the Mareotic Lake! These required allegiance to Leviathan in their piscine theology. Whether moon, Mars or some fictitious place in the standoff of distortion and convention, to paraphrasts Old Town was a marine museum. A Greece emptied of its whales. A thousand springs flow into this ake against thought and forethought. Leviathan in its Mardi Gras trades in masks and scales. They build their huts like him as a home. So their idea of life could be complete. It's one thing

401

to polyploid a cow three times life size, too big for a Mack truck. All these are shadows of the real work of quantum codes, cables and call signs, but this technology in the wild accounts for the giant size also of Behemoth, like a tetraployed elephant.

Because they had not seen the Lev their buildings took on shapes of eels, whales, squid, materia proxima, materia remota, materia ultima. These new mystical men prove the history of the Odyssey. As Behmists of the slabby mists might purl ecstatic chapters of perfection of crystal streams over rock and ledge, or balsam pine hid in the small caves of hillside with natural springs, Aurora hid in their language its universal matrix and Philologus esoteria prefigured. The great deliverance they felt was soon to be displayed. Not to deny fish mystics and Baptists worldwide, invisible storehouse of diverse mythmakers, that collective fiction that fathers early and later times to enable government, is followers virulent in self interest lept at the Behemoth dish while down at the other lept Leviathan, chief magistrate unlike any man today.

# Fodder

By Emily Bilman

His other self milked the ewe
on the meadow in the spring
of their contentment.

They roamed right above
the town's rooftops patterned
in uneven tiled geometries.

In the greenness of his mind
he offered clover, grain and grass
to the sheep in the pasture.

His other self watched as if
a bond of blood united them
while the fodder turned to milk.

# Witching Hour

By Tal Garmiza

This is my witching hour.
At midnight Gravity will draw me
into my power.
I welcome the night
with flames of fire;
This is my witching hour.

As I bath in chaos created by me,
I find myself growing into everything
I ever wished to be.
Time is meaningless and finally I can see,
so I laugh with my fears
and I set my tears free.

This is my witching hour.
The moonlight will throw me
into my power.
Surprisingly enough
I will find comfort in my own skin,
I am whole tonight when everything is in between.

# Therapy is the Most Punk Rock

By Shannon Frost Greenstein

Punk is rage, red hot magma violently simmering

beneath the surface;

uncontainable fury at an establishment that labels

all punk rockers as the "other."


Punk is combat, the all-encompassing struggle for

that ultimate "fuck you,"

the fight for generational change made manifest;

and the future an empty unknown.


Punk is a quest, an epic journey of

terror and wrath

while the world continues to turn

as if this crusade is not currently raging.


Punk is power, the clout to quiet an entire room

and its collective judgment;

dropped jaws and second glances and whispered comments

at the dominion to be different.


Punk is strength, a Sisyphean effort to continue; the

Darwinian drive

to endure and persist;

Nietzschean Will to Power incarnate

and survival through sheer grit.

Punk is radical honesty, lost and adrift in

a sea of inauthenticity;

the courage to live one's own Truth

whatever the cost.

Therapy is all these things and more. It is triumph over self-
destruction

and a brain without serotonin.

It is a painful commitment to build a life worth living,

because therapy is the *most* punk rock.

# A Most Unusual House

By Linda Imbler

An unusual house, the original one.
The only one of its kind begun.
Built with old wood grown long in the past,
Old lumber, second-hand, but strong enough to last.

All walls, floors, shelves built back then,
Just frozen messages left by dead men.
They put a few possessions to the fore,
Used the rest of the space as a memories' store.

And even after these owners went away,
The caretakers assigned to conserve it, they
Maintained it in a durable, well-kept state.
It was meant to have a long-term fate.

A house set back on a tree-lined street,
With perfect angled corners where two walls meet.
All man's love, beauty and peace here to see.
Historic wooden windows fitted beautifully.

No wicked machines within to be found,
Just a few beautiful things, 5 books leather bound,
5 marble statues upon pedestals held,
5 oils on the walls, all parallel.

It hasn't changed much over time.
To tear it down would be a crime.
An owner with few material needs would rejoice,
Enamored with 15 visual selections of choice.

# A Ramble on Depression

By Ruchira Mandal

The earth and we were born of the same smothered ashes.
Like attracts like. So you'll know what I mean when
I speak of days when gravity holds my feet across memorized
paths
I've crossed a thousand times in fitful sleep. Sometimes,
It seems easier to be a rock.

I've been in rooms stretched across separate planets
Like an asteroid off its orbit. But the air and I
Were born of the same expansion, and it
Clung to me like an ebbing tide, never
Letting go.

There are paths around the sun, and paths inside your head.
None of it leads anywhere.
I wonder if the earth ever feels lost.

# Building in the Wind

By Tal Garmiza.

Buildings don't fly in the wind.
They stay where they are
so those who live inside of them
won't be scared to exist.

The wind shall whisper at night
through the edges of the doors,
telling then 'she' can see them,
'she' knows the better than all.

In the morning after the storm will appear-
sand in each street;
and people inside their coats hiding,
hiding from the wind.

At night the wind will call them,
and they are brave and they are weak;
They hide the temptation each day,
and buildings don't fly in the wind.

# Rooftops

By Jude Brigley

# Hope

By Stephen Craig Finlay

I think of the deadening grass, brown. Full of
November. How it lays thick and straight as a
thatched roof arching down toward the creek.
The sort of roof I marveled over in a book that
showed cutaways of castles and homes people
lived in centuries ago, when everything was
handmade and at least as different as breath. If
you love the worn footprints in a marble
staircase how can you not be thrown into
euphoria by the sight of a river? I think of the
eddies and movement of brown water that
slides beneath those rusting rail bridges across
the Spoon River, and how when Edgar Lee
Masters wrote about it he made it seem as if
the towns they built the bridges for were
already so worn and tattered. I think of the
shuttered storefronts of these little drive
through valley towns now, boarded up decades
already when I was young. And I remember
that the last thing to escape Pandora's box was
Hope.

# Contributors

**A Whittenberg** is a Philadelphia native who has a global perspective. If she wasn't an author she'd be a private detective or a jazz singer. She loves reading about history and true crime. Her other novels include *Sweet Thang, Hollywood and Maine, Life is Fine, Tutored* and *The Sane Asylum.*

**AE Reiff** is a poet of Philadelphia. He has written The True Light that Lights (Parousia Reads, 2020) and Encouragements for Such as Shall Have Intention to be Undertakers in the Planting (Austin, 1973).

**Anagha Joy**, a freelance researcher. I am 26 years of age. Completed Graduation from Osmania University and secured fourth rank both for UG and PG in the University. Worked as a Lecturer in a Women's College @ Hyderabad for a period of one year. I had also published three articles in an UGC-Approved journal. Writing and scribbling in accordance to the flow of my mind is my passion.

**Anannya Dasgupta** is a poet and visual artist who lives in Chennai, India.

**Ann Privateer** is a poet, artist, and photographer. Some of her work has appeared in Third Wednesday, Manzanita, and Entering to name a few.

**B.A. Brittingham** Formerly of New York City and South Florida, Brittingham is currently a resident of Southwestern Michigan, and a writer with an interest in photography.

**Beatrice Georgalidis** is the executive director of New York's Bright Hill Press, a literary art center and gallery. She has worked for more than twenty years in film and television as a writer, producer and videographer for many companies including Sundance Channel, MTV, VH1.

**Bill Cushing** Called the "blue collar poet" by peers at the University of Central Florida, Bill Cushing moved to California by way of Puerto Rico after earning his MFA from Goddard College. His book, A Former Life, was released in 2019 and was recently honored with a Kops-Featherling International Book Award.

**Bransha Gautier** is an award-winning visual artist and photographer, based in Vienna. With hundreds of exhibitions Bransha's art can be found in numerous permanent and private collections of museums worldwide.

**Bruce McRae**, a Canadian musician currently residing on Salt Spring Island BC, is a multiple Pushcart nominee with over 1,600 poems published internationally in magazines such as Poetry, Rattle and the North American Review. His books are 'The So-Called Sonnets' (Silenced Press); 'An Unbecoming Fit Of Frenzy'; (Cawing Crow Press); 'Like As If' (Pski's Porch); 'Hearsay' (The Poet's Haven).

**C. Rose Widmann** (they/them) is a senior at Michigan State University majoring in Theater and English. In their free time they are a freelance artist and avid bookworm.

**Carl "Papa" Palmer** of Old Mill Road in Ridgeway, Virginia, lives in University Place, Washington.He is retired from the military and Federal Aviation Administration (FAA) enjoying life as "Papa"to his grand descendants and being a Franciscan Hospice volunteer. Carl is a Pushcart Prize, Best of the Net and Micro Award nominee.   PAPA's MOTTO: Long Weekends Forever!

**Carmen Caro** Master in Plastic and visual artist from Bogotá, Colombia, focused con social art with communities from violent and war locations. She involves in dynamics regarding resistance processes from the body, language and territorial or vernacular dynamics. Her field-based research has been published in Spain, Mexico and Colombia. Her work resonates inside the collective art spectrum, gentrification impact and sensitization methodologies for the appropriation of violated and endangered territories. The present work presents the last photos of the SER, Space for education and Reconciliation where 600 ex FARC soldiers were living, now this territory is empty due to the increasing murders of social lieders enhanced by the isolation and silence conditions developed after Covid 19.

**Catherine Alexander** A Pushcart Prize and Best of the Net nominee, Catherine Alexander has published stories in 42 literary journals and anthologies. Her work has been aired on NPR by Paul Auster, and performed in LA Word Theatre. She has taught fiction at the University of Washington and Edmonds College for fifteen years. Currently teaching privately in Seattle, she has completed a short story collection, a novel, Dogs Don't Cook, and working on another book.

**Chahat Soneja**: In the past few years, I have explored and worked across quite a few mediums and materials, drawing and painting portraits of women and other daily life experiences that I have on a day-to-day basis, working with photography, text, installations, collaborative wall art and site-specific projects. I often come across the beauty of portraying what is already around but which is often ignored or not considered beautiful or paid less attention towards, usually the mundane. That is, my surroundings, with different objects, nature, and people realizing the importance of the often ignored people, environment, and objects which I found within the margin of beautiful in the ordinary and portrayed them outside of their general usage. Finding the aesthetics and the "not normal" in daily surroundings, I have made drawings of the same. Through my works, I hope to give a new meaning to the mundane, often ignored objects, people and surroundings. I hope to find joy while portraying the boring or ignored. This way I come up with a range of original ideas and theories. In the works attached I intend to portray the same along with showing the challenges that come along with the corona virus pandemic.

**CJP Lee** is an artist and academic the author/editor of 20 books, including The Psychology of Screenwriting (Bloomsbury). Lee is Fellow of the Royal Society of Art, Professor of Film, and winner of the Aesthetica Prize. Recent art in Tentacular and the Open Space Gallery. Website https://cjplee.com

**Dave Medd** was born in Hull in 1951 and moved to Northumberland in 1969. His work has been published in Poetry North East, Outposts, Orbis, Dream Catcher and The Coffee House and on I Am Not A Silent Poet and The Cicerone Journal. He now lives and writes in Rothbury.

**David Subacchi** lives in Wales (UK) where he was born of Italian roots. He studied at the University of Liverpool and his diverse background (he writes in English, Welsh and Italian) significantly influences his writing. David has six published collections of his poetry and you can find out more about him at https://www.writeoutloud.net/profiles/davidsubacchi

**Dee Allen** African-Italian performance poet based in Oakland, California. Active on the creative writing & Spoken Word tips since the early 1990s. Author of 5 books [ Boneyard, Unwritten Law, Stormwater and Skeletal Black, all from POOR Press, and from Conviction 2 Change Publishing, Elohi Unitsi ] under his figurative belt so far.

**Derek Roper** has dedicated his creativity and ingenuity to the cosmic mythos. The Mad Artist focuses much of his work on the mysteries of comic horror. Some of his favorite classic cosmic horror stories include the Call of Cthulhu, The Shadow Over Innsmouth, and the King in Yellow. His passion for these stories and the mythos drive his creative processes. Derek primarily works with digital art, but also has a passion for clay work and wood burning. He is always working with new mediums to portray his art.

**Douglas K Currier** lives in Carlisle, PA with his wife. He is a graduate of the University of Pittsburgh MFA program and has published poetry and fiction in Spanish and English in North and South America. His fiction has appeared in Otherwise Engaged, Trajectory, and Bandit Fiction.

**Dr. Emily Bilman** is London Poetry Society's Stanza representative in Geneva where she lives and teaches poetry. Her dissertation, *The Psychodynamics of Poetry,* was published by Lambert Academic in 2010 and *Modern Ekphrasis* in 2013 by Peter Lang, CH. Three poetry books, *A Woman By A Well, Resilience, and The Threshold of Broken Waters* were published by Troubador, UK in 2015 and the latest in 2018. Her poems, essays, and translations of Neruda and Valéry appeared in *The Battersea Review, Hunger Mountain, The High Window, The Journal of Poetics Research, Tuck Magazine, Offshoots, Expanded Field, The London Magazine, and MONK.* "*The Tear-Catcher*" won the first prize for depth poetry in The New York Literary Magazine. She edits and writes poems and essays for an digital ekphrastic publication www.paintedpoetry.org. Her latest poetry book, *The Threshold of Broken Waters,* was published by Troubador in September 2018. Her short fiction piece "The Gun" appeared in *Talking Soup.* She blogs on her website: http://www.emiliebilman.wix.com/emily-bilman

**Dr. Shubha Dwivedi** is a poet and translator. She teaches English at Atma Ram Sanatan Dharma College, University of Delhi, India.

**Elena Brooke** I am a 24-year-old writer from Manchester, UK. I have been writing fiction stories from a young age, and I am currently interested in exploring the impact of people meeting with other, and connecting with them on a personal level.

**Eva Eliav** received a BA in English Lang and Lit from The University of Toronto and completed her studies towards an MA in English and American Literature at the University of Tel Aviv. Her poetry and short fiction have been published in numerous literary journals both online and in print, including Room, The St. Ann's Review, Emrys Journal, Ilanot Review, Flashquake, The Apple Valley Review, Stand Magazine, The Blue Nib, Horizon Review, Boston Literary Magazine, The Enchanted Conversation, Constellations and Fictive Dream. Her poetry collection, Eve, was published in spring 2019 by Red Bird Chapbooks. She has a poetry chapbook forthcoming from Kelsay Books.

**F. Berna Uysal,** a feminist and a bibliophile, is an Istanbul born and raised academic in literature. She is a baby storyteller and a coffee enthusiast. Her curiosity is on psychoanalytical criticism in literature and magical realism now because as Sartre states; "L'enfer cest les autres".

**Faruk Buzhala** is a well-known poet from Ferizaj, Kosovo. He was born in 9 March 1968 in Pristina. He is the former menager and leader of "De Rada" a literary association, from 2012 till 2018, and also the representer of Kosovo on 100 TPC organization. Except poems, he also writes short stories, essays, literary reviews, traveltales, etc. Faruk Buzhala is a organizer and manager of many events that are kept in Ferizaj city. His poems are translated in English, Italian, Spanish, French, German, Croatian and Chinese language, and are published in a couple anthologies such in USA, Italy, Mexico, Albania, China, etc. He has published five books: " Qeshje Jokeriane"(Jokerian Smile) 1998, " Shtëpia pa rrugë "(House without road) 2009, " Njeriu me katër hije "(Man with four shadows) 2012, " Shkëlqim verbërues"(Blinding brilliance) 2015, and "Një gur mangut"(A stone less) 2018.

**Guilherme Bortoluzzi** is a artist and landscape designer, that explore the relations between man and the nature that sprouts in urban areas.

**Helga Grundler-Schierloh** is a bilingual writer with a journalism degree. My work has appeared in the USA, the UK, and Canada. My debut novel, Burying Leo, a MeToo story released in 2017, won second place in women's fiction during Pen Craft Awards' 2018 writing contest.

**Jaina Cipriano** Photographer - Set Designer - Writer - Director

**Jan Ball** has had 319 poems published or accepted in journals in the U.S., Australia, Great Britain, Canada, Czech Republic, India and Ireland in journals like: Atlanta Review, Chiron, Main Street Rag, and Poets&Artists. Her two chapbooks and first full-length poetry book, I Wanted To Dance With My Father, were published by Finishing Line Press. Her poem, "Not Sharing at Yoshu" has just been nominated for the Pushcart by Orbis, Great Britain, 2020. Jan and her husband travel a lot but like to cook for friends when they are home in Chicago.

**JBMulligan** has published more than 1100 poems and stories in various magazines over the past 45 years, and has had two chapbooks: The Stations of the Cross and THIS WAY TO THE EGRESS, as well as 2 e-books: The City of Now and Then, and A Book of Psalms (a loose translation). He has appeared in more than a dozen anthologies.

**Jeanette Willert** Recent Vice-President of the Alabama State Poetry Society and their 2018 Poet of the Year. Her chapbook *Appalachia, Amour* won the Morris Chapbook Award (2017), Her poems are in a variety of journals and anthologies. Her first poetry book *it was never Eden* (Negative Capability Press) will debut in a few months.

**Jeffrey G. Delfin** is a graduate of AB Mass Communication at Far Eastern University way back in 1999. He is a Teacher, Writer, and Photographer and hailed as one of the grand prize winners of The League of Poets' "A Song of Peace" an international poetry writing contest.

**Jenn Powers** is a writer and visual artist from New England. She is currently at work on a mystery thriller. She has work published or forthcoming in over 70 literary journals, including *Hayden's Ferry Review, The Pinch, Jabberwock Review, Thin Air Magazine, Calyx, Spillway, CutBank, Witness, Gemini,* and *Lunch Ticket.* Her work has been anthologized with Running Wild Press, Kasva Press, and Scribes Valley Publishing, and she's been nominated for the Pushcart Prize, Best of the Net, and Best Small Fictions. Please visit www.jennpowers.com for more information.

**John Grey** is an Australian poet, US resident. Recently published in Soundings East, Dalhousie Review and Qwerty with work upcoming in West Trade Review, Willard and Maple and Connecticut River Review.

**John Tavares** Born and raised in Sioux Lookout, Ontario, John is the son of Portuguese immigrants from the Azores. His education includes graduation from 2-year GAS at Humber College in Etobicoke with concentration in psychology (1993), 3-year journalism at Centennial College in East York (1996) and the Specialized Honors BA in English from York University in North York (2012). He worked as a research assistant for the Sioux Lookout Public Library and as a research assistant in waste management for the SLKT public works department and regional recycle association. He also worked for persons with disabilities at the Sioux Lookout Association for Community Living.

**Jude Brigley** is Welsh. She has been a teacher an editor and a performance poet. She is now writing more for the page. Her poems and prose pieces have been published in a plethora of magazines, including *Blue Ink, Ariel Chart, Affinity* and *Ink and Nebula.*

***K. P. Heyming*** is a bilingual, Canadian writer with a yearning to set her soul in ink and paper. Fiercely driven to ensnare all of life's little moments, she works tirelessly for her passion so that she may someday lead others to find their own meaning in her words.

**K.A. Johnson** has a BA in English/Journalism with a minor in Classics from The University of New Hampshire. He covered the news in the small New Hampshire college town of Durham for The New Hampshire before ditching the snow and moving south to Richmond, Virginia, where he lives with his wife Jennifer and his two furry writing partners Sparta Jesus Vernal-Johnson and Kolby Catmatix Domitian Johnson. www.kenjohnsonwrites.com (website and blog) @kenjohnsontnh (Twitter)

**Karol Nielsen** is the author of the memoirs Black Elephants (Bison Books, 2011) and Walking A&P (Mascot Books, 2018) and the chapbooks This Woman I Thought I'd Be (Finishing Line Press, 2012) and Vietnam Made Me Who I Am (Finishing Line Press, 2020). Her first memoir was shortlisted for the William Saroyan International Prize for Writing in nonfiction in 2012. Her full poetry collection was a finalist for the Colorado Prize for Poetry in 2007. Her work has appeared in Epiphany, Guernica, Lumina, North Dakota Quarterly, Permafrost, RiverSedge, and elsewhere. She has taught writing at New York University and New York Writers Workshop.

**Kelli J Gavin** of Carver, Minnesota is a Writer, Editor, Blogger and Professional Organizer. Her work can be found with Clarendon House Publishing, Sweetycat Press, The Ugly Writers, Sweatpants & Coffee, Zombie Pirates Publishing, Setu, Cut 19, Passionate Chic, Otherwise Engaged, Flora Fiction, Love What Matters, Printed Words and Southwest Media among others. Kelli's first two books were released in 2019 ("I Regret Nothing- A Collection of Poetry and Prose" and "My Name is Zach- A Teenage Perspective on Autism"). She has also co-authored 17 anthology books. Her blog can be found at www.kellijgavin.blogspot.com .

**Lee Ellis** lives in Surfside Beach, TX where, in addition to writing, she rescues birds and transports injured feathered and furred critters to rehabilitators. She has published in Pearl literary magazine, the Life in the Time online project, and Odes and Elegies: Ecopoetry from the Gulf Coast.

**Linda Imbler** is the author of five paperback poetry collections and three e-book collections (Soma Publishing.) This writer lives in Wichita, Kansas with her husband, Mike the Luthier, several quite intelligent saltwater fish, and an ever-growing family of gorgeous guitars. Learn more at lindaspoetryblog.blogspot.com.

**Linda M. Crate** has been published in numerous magazines. Linda's authored seven poetry chapbooks, the latest being: *the samurai* (Yellow Arrow Publishing, October 2020), and three full-length poetry collections: *Vampire Daughter* (Dark Gatekeeper Gaming, February 2020), *The Sweetest Blood* (Cyberwit, February 2020), and *Mythology of My Bones* (Cyberwit, August 2020).

**Lorraine Caputo** Poet-translator-travel writer Lorraine Caputo's works appear in over 200 journals on six continents; and 12 chapbooks of poetry – including *Caribbean Nights* (Red Bird Chapbooks) and *On Galápagos Shores* (dancing girl press). She travels through Latin America, listening to the voices of the pueblos and Earth.

**M. A. Blickley** is a widely published author of fiction, nonfiction, poetry and drama. Blickley is a proud member of the Dramatists Guild and PEN American Center whose most recent book is a text-based art collaboration with fine arts photographer Amy Bassin, *Dream Streams*. (Clare Songbirds Publishing House).

**Madeleine McDonald** lives in Yorkshire, England, where the cliffs crumble in to the sea. She finds inspiration walking on the beach before the world wakes up.

**Mae Tanes Espada** studied English and majored in Anglo-American literature during her undergraduate years. She's now pursuing Law while teaching arts and humanities subjects in senior high school. After a couple of years, she aspires to become a rainforest. She currently lives in the Philippines.

**Mark A. Fisher** is a writer, poet, and playwright living in Tehachapi, CA. His poetry has appeared in: riverbabble, Spectrum, Silver Blade, Penumbra, Lummox, and many other places. His first chapbook, drifter, is available from Amazon. His second, hour of lead, won the 2017 San Gabriel Valley Poetry Chapbook Contest

**Mark Andrew Heathcote** is adult learning difficulties support worker, his poetry has been published in many journals, magazines and anthologies, he resides in the UK, from Manchester, he is the author of "In Perpetuity" and "Back on Earth" two books of poems published by a CTU publishing group ~ Creative Talents Unleashed

**Martin Eastland** Born and raised in Glasgow, Martin Eastland has been writing for 30 years, first being published in 2019 and after in several indie publications. Currently, his solo collection of short suspense-horror stories sits under consideration from a US publisher. He lives with his two young sons in Shropshire, England.

**Matthew Kerr** is a writer and co-creator of The Working Experience podcast. The Working Experience explores issues related to work and interviews guests such as authors, filmmakers, politicians and witches to better understand the process by which they do their jobs.

**Mike L. Nichols** is a graduate of Idaho State University and a recipient of the Ford Swetnam Poetry Prize. He lives and writes in Eastern Idaho. Look for his poetry in *Rogue Agent, Tattoo Highway, Ink&Nebula, Plainsongs Magazine,* and elsewhere. Look for his work in Underground Voices, Black Rock & Sage, The Literary Nest, The Blue Nib and elsewhere. Find more at deadgirldancing.net

**Neal Amandus Gellaco** is a Filipino writer and an undergraduate student of Psychology in the University of the Philippines Diliman where he also takes up cognate courses in Creative Writing and Comparative Literature.

**Ololade Akinlabi Ige** is a young Nigerian poet, a graduate of Obafemi Awolowo University (OAU). He was a nominee for Nigeria Writers Award 2017 and was shortlisted for Albert Jungan poetry prize in 2018. He won the 2018 Ken Egba Poetry prize organized by Poet in Nigeria (PIN). His works have featured in Muse for world peace anthology, 84 delicious bottles of wine for Wole Soyinka, Word Rhymes and Rhythm (WRR) anthology, Sabr Literary Magazine, Wreath for a Wayfarer, Songs of peace anthology among others. He is the author of the novel, Ocean of Tears.

**Peniel Gifted** is a young Nigerian poet and writer. She has great enthusiasm for reading, writing and learning and also an adroit lover of nature and God's word.

**Perla Kantarjian** is a Lebanese-Armenian writer, editor, journalist, and instructor from Beirut. Her works have appeared in multiple journals and platforms, including Rebelle Society, Bookstr, Rusted Radishes, Annahar Newspaper, The Armenian Weekly, Walqalam, and more.

**Rachel Makinson** is a writer.

**RAMEEZ AHMAD BHAT** Research Student Aligarh Muslim University

**Rob Mimpriss** is the author of three short story collections, the editor of Dangerous Asylums, an anthology of fiction inspired by the history of Denbigh Mental Hospital, a translator of Welsh literature, and a member of the Welsh Academy. He lives in Bangor, Wales, and at www.robmimpriss.com.

**Robert Cooperman**'s latest collection is THE GHOSTS AND BONES OF TROY (Kelsay Books). Forthcoming from Finishing Line Press is the chapbook ALL OUR FARE-THEE-WELLS.

**Rp Verlaine** lives and writes in New York City. He has an MFA in creative writing from City College. He taught in New York Public schools for many years. Retired from teaching, he continues to write and do photography in New York. He had a volume of poetry- Damaged by Dames & Drinking published in 2017 and another – Femme Fatales Movie Starlets & Rockers in 2018. A set of three e-books began with the publication of Lies From The Autobiography vol1 was published in November of 2018. Vol 2 was published in 2019 and a third Volume in 2020.

**Ruchira Mandal** lives in kolkata and likes to hide inside books and songs. She wanted to be a superhero but since that gig didn't work out, she writes instead. You can follow her on Twitter @RucchiraM snd on Instagram @ruchirarambles

**Shaista Fazal** is passionate writer who writes, writes and writes! Shaista is a short story writer, blogger, copywriter, ghost writer of books, article writer... you name it.
Shaista's writing has been featured in several publications and has won several short story contests.

**Shannon Frost Greenstein** is the author of "Pray for Us Sinners", a fiction collection from Alien Buddha Press, and "More.", a poetry collection by Wild Pressed Books. She is a Pushcart Prize nominee and a former Ph.D. candidate in Continental Philosophy. Follow her at shannonfrostgreenstein.com or on Twitter at @ShannonFrostGre.

**Sohini Shabnam** from India Sohini is a student of 2nd year, English honours. Sohini hobbies are- writing, drawing, photography, gardening and doing many other artistic things.

**Stephen Craig Finlay** Library Director, Murray State College

**Steven Rossi** began writing to connect with spirituality, fellow people, and the world. He currently lives in Washington, D.C. and loves exploring the city. When he's not at his consulting job, you can find him at his Buddhist temple, going to concerts and finding the best cafes in town.

**Sumati Muniandy** is currently an educator and a writer. She holds her Master's Degree in TESOL from University Southern Queensland, Business Administration from University Putra Malaysia (UPM), Diploma in TESL from Maktab Perguruan Ipoh and Diploma in TESOL from London Teacher Training College. She has written a number of articles on various topics in The Star and New Straits Times. She has also presented papers in conferences. Writing is her passion and she writes her real life experiences to inspire others. She believes that everyone has a story to tell.

**Swarnav Misra** is a student of English Literature with a keen interest in Indian medieval history. At present, he is doing his BA from St. Edmund's College in Shillong, India. Not a professional or refined poet, but likes to engage in the uncurbed flow of emotions in the vibrant canvas of creation.

**Tal Garmiza** I am an Israeli poet and multidisciplinary artist that creates both in English and Hebrew. If one of the texts might be right I would love to know. They were published online only before.

**Tali Cohen Shabtai**, is a poet, she was born in Jerusalem, Israel. She began writing poetry at the age of six, she had been an excellent student of literature. She began her writings by publishing her impressions in the school's newspaper. First of all she published her poetry in a prestigious literary magazine of Israel 'Moznayim' when she was fifteen years old.Tali has written three poetry books: "Purple Diluted in a Black's Thick", (bilingual 2007), "Protest" (bilingual 2012) and "Nine Years From You" (2018).Tali's poems expresses spiritual and physical exile. She is studying her exile and freedom paradox, her cosmopolitan vision is very obvious in her writings. She lived some years in Oslo Norway and in the U.S.A. She is very prominent as a poet with a special lyric, "she doesn't give herself easily, but subject to her own rules".Tali studied at the "David Yellin College of Education" for a bachelor's degree. She is a member of the Hebrew Writers Association and the Israeli Writers Association in the state of Israel.In 2014, Cohen Shabtai also participated in a Norwegian documentary about poets' lives called "The Last Bohemian"- "Den Siste Bohemien",and screened in the cinema in Scandinavia. By 2020, her fourth book of poetry will be published which will also be published in Norway. Her literary works have been translated into many languages as well.

**Thomas Zampino** is an attorney in private practice in New York City. Formerly with *Patheos*, he now writes poems and reflections at *The Catholic Conspiracy*. His poems have appeared or will soon appear in *Bard's Annual 2019*, *Bard's Annual 2020*, *Trees in a Garden of Ashes* (2020), *Otherwise Engaged* (2020), *The University of Chicago Memoryhouse Magazine* (2020), *Chaos, A Poetry Vortex* (2020), *The Walt Whitman Collaborative Project* (2020), *Nassau County Voices in Verse* (2020), twice in *Verse-Virtual* (an on-line anthology), and a video production of *Precise Moment* by Gui Agustini. He is also working on a book of poetry tentatively scheduled for 2021.

**William Barker** (1978- ) was born in Ridgewood, New Jersey and currently resides in Hawthorne, New Jersey with his wife, two boys, and black cat, Ziggy Stardust. Writing since adolescence, he fell in love with poetry in 2006 after a lifetime of misunderstanding and judging the form, wrongly. He has independently produced two full-length books of poetry entitled: Shards (poems 2007-2010) and Workhorse (poems 2012-2015) as well as two chapbooks: The Writing Must Leap Upon You Like a Wild Beast (2012) and Sleeping Children Are Still Flying (2015). Recently, his poetry appeared in Anthology's by Silver Birch Press (2013) and Perpetual Motion Machine Publishing (2014), as well as Dragonfly Magazine (2020) and Heroin Love Songs (2020). Mr. Barker's third full-length book of poetry, Blue Sunday, is nearly complete. He is also currently working on a trilogy of novels, with several other poetry projects forthcoming as well.

**Yeshi Choden**. I am from Bhutan. I am 26 years old and currently undertaking Post Graduate Diploma in Public Administration at the Royal Institute of Management in Thimphu. By the time the journal issue gets published, I would have completed the training and be employed in the civil service. I have a Bachelor's degree in English Studies from Royal Thimphu College. I love to indulge in food, music, movies, ideas, words.

Printed in Great Britain
by Amazon